Lab

Throughout his career, **Charles Seliger** (American, 1926–2009) pursued an inner world of organic abstraction, celebrating the structural complexities of natural forms. Inspired by a wide range of literature in natural history, biology, and physics, he cultivated a poetic style of abstraction that explored the dynamics of order and chaos animating the celestial, geographical, and biological realms. Seliger paid homage to nature's infinite variety and his paintings have been described as "microscopic views of the natural world".

Born in New York City but raised in Jersey City, Seliger never completed high school or received formal art training. In 1943, he befriended artist Jimmy Ernst and was quickly drawn into the circle of avant-garde artists championed by Howard Putzel and Peggy Guggenheim. Two years later, at the age of nineteen, Seliger was included in the groundbreaking 67 Gallery exhibition *A Problem for Critics*, and had his first solo show at Guggenheim's Art of This Century gallery. At the time, Seliger was the youngest artist exhibiting with members of the abstract expressionist movement, and he was only twenty years old when the Museum of Modern Art acquired his painting *Natural History: Form within Rock* (1946). In 1950, Seliger obtained representation from Willard Gallery, forming close friendships with artists Mark Tobey, Lyonel Feininger, and Norman Lewis. By 1949, Seliger had his first major museum exhibition at the de Young Memorial Museum, San Francisco. During his lifetime, his art was celebrated in over forty-five solo shows at prominent galleries in New York and Europe. In 1986, Seliger was given his first retrospective at the Solomon R. Guggenheim Museum, which now holds the largest collection of his work. His work is also represented in numerous public institutions including the Metropolitan Museum of Art, the Museum of Modern Art, and the Whitney Museum of American Art. In 2003, Seliger received the Pollock-Krasner Foundation's Lee Krasner Award in recognition of his long and illustrious career in the arts. In 2005, the Morgan Library and Museum acquired his journals – 148 hand-written volumes produced between 1952 to 2009. In 2012, the Mint Museum in Charlotte, North Carolina organized the traveling exhibition *Seeing the World Within: Charles Seliger in the 1940s*.

Labyrinthed
Poems

DAVID JAFFIN

First published in the United Kingdom in 2012 by
Shearsman Books
50 Westons Hill Drive
Emersons Green
Bristol BS16 7DF

Shearsman Books Ltd Registered Office
30–31 St. James Place, Mangotsfield, Bristol BS16 9JB
(this address not for correspondence)

www.shearsman.com

ISBN 978-1-84861-244-0

Distributed for Shearsman Books in the U. S. A.
by Small Press Distribution, 1341 Seventh Avenue, Berkeley, CA 94710
E-Mail orders@spdbooks.org
www.spdbooks.org

Production, composition & cover design: Edition Wortschatz, an imprint of
Neufeld Verlag, Schwarzenfeld/Germany
E-Mail info@edition-wortschatz.de

Title picture:
Charles Seliger (1926–2009)
Ways of Nature: 17 (detail), 2008
acrylic, Micron pen, colored pencil, matte gel,
and beeswax varnish on gessoed Masonite
16″ x 20″, signed and dated
Courtesy of Michael Rosenfield Gallery, LLC, New York, NY
www.michaelrosenfeldart.com

Printed in Germany

Contents

7

8

11

I've been often asked why I break words
between lines. As Lenore, one of my most
perceptive readers said, "You don't really break
words between lines, but place them within
the entire rhythmic flow of the poem."

As my poems are extremely condensed I don't
want words, especially the longer ones, to be
"hanging out", therefore this very musical need
for such a continuing on. Word-break, if one
wants to call it that, means that these words
must be put back together again, almost as if
they've become recreated, newly realized.

David Jaffin

The unsaid

may lead a

life-of-its-
own gnawing

at the very
bastions of

our own self-
defenses.

"Viel Feinde viel Ehr"

(the more enemies the more honor)

but those

most-of-all
enemies em

bedded deeply
within oursel

ves claiming
a voice that

would uncall
whatever peace-

of-mind we'
ve tentative

ly been hold
ing on-to

despite them.

Labyrinthed

as a fly

caught in a
spider's web

the more he
tried the dee

per he became
entangled

in that no-
ways-out.

For those

who try lead

ing other per
son's lives

(especial
ly those of

their child
ren) It may

be a vain at
tempt at find

ing a way out-
of-their-own.

When this

all-prevad

ing green land
scapes an

Easter of its
own thorough

ly-attuned
blessing

s.

John 21

Peter and
the other

disciple
s caught no

thing while
returning

to their old
way of life

Fishermen
until nett

ed again in
Christ's o

ther-kind-
of-catch.

Easter-past

daily rout

ined yet an
unseen silent

ly revealing
inwardly o

ther-light.

Prayer

is only when

our own voice
overheard

by another.

Soft spring

raining the

slightly color
ed fragran

ce of these
touched-to-

birth flower
ing time

s.

The fresh

ly-light

green leave
s wetted to

the muted
silences of

their still
shadow

ing reflect
ions.

Do we read

poems or do

they read us
through–

touching
those unknown

depths of in
wardly respon

sive quiet
udes.

Pre-forming

The empty-out

lives of pre-
forming house

s as some per
sons I've known

naked and a
lone to the

where of
their not-yet

walled-in
shadowing

s.

The becomings

We'll never

really know
the becoming

s their how
and why-like

clay form
ing more its

in-discover
ing hand-reach

ing design
s.

Life contin

ually becom

ing the more
of his be

ing depriv
ed of a

voice he
could bare

ly distin
guish as his

own.

A. B.

His life pre–

deciding
that one-way

street of
his right coll

ege wife pro
fession until

all those hope
s and dream

s of his
dead-ended

a nicely car
ved remem

brance-stone.

Spring'

s also a

season of
the mind a

wakening
out of the

cold and
barren fro

zen-down
earth seed

ed to its
once and

only-timed
renewal.

Juggling

colored ball

s until their
severall

ed height
s kept his

hands realiz
ing those

momentary
interval

s of their
ground-de

scending
causes.

The winter

ed bird's
short-stop

flight's a
wareness

of why those
reaching

mountain
s still high

er than their
continuing

instinct for
warmth.

Weathered

Have we been

too often
weathered

sky-depend
ently cloud-

darkening
the inner

reach of our
soundless

response.

This only-now

Coming from

opposite dir
ections

we met–at–the
middle of

those decid
ing question

s as if the
routes we'd

taken (how
ever varied)

had predeter
mined this

only-now.

Our side of

We often real

ize only our
side of as

if all truth
s weren't

shadowed
by those o

ther length
s of readied

denials.

Even humour

can be un

evenly reali
zed Why this

and not that
smile perhap

s conceal
ing a blank-

stop when
life's train'

s continu
ally pass

ing on.

Is language

an extens

ion of our
most person

al express
ion Or is it

often re-rout
ed to the

far-beyond'
s of its

newly reali
zed cleansed-

being.

Seen through

For years

he saw those
poems through

the same win
dow until one

day he reali
zed that glass

was looking
him back.

A poem is

when language

becomes more
of the mean

ing than that
preempted

idea or fully–
felt–feel.

For Rosemarie

Our friend

s (so diverse
as they are) cir

cling the many
sides of where

we've been
centered

for a togeth
ered–unity-

of–self.

Pontius Pilate's

"what is

truth" as if
one could see

it this way
or that both

ways at once
Jesus stand

ing a higher
ground realiz

ing where one
can't see at

all Cyclopsed
to the death–

guarantee
of man's self–

evolving way
s.

If one

could create

love or the
death of

death's un
failing claim

s one could
create the

world as well
turning u

pon its pre–
given axis.

Evil'

s not only

a person but
a place hid

den somewhere
deeply with

in those un
known realm

s of our
self–being.

The 10 Commandments

He set the

boundar
ies to those

earth-game
s of our

playing out
side the rule

s praying
to other god

s in their
earth-attir

ed power-
claims.

Moralizers

Those who

moralize
the most like

ly candidat
es for that

swelling pit
of under

ground instin
ctual fall

ings.

Pink

resolving

to pursue
a better life

donned those
bestly embroi

dered cloth
es of his

better-con
scienced

uprightness
medalled

with pawned
awards of

more distin
guished per

sonages.

Those grand ideas

When those

grand ideas
took hold of

his powerful
ly thought-

through be
ing system

ed to less
er weight

ed flesh and
boned-in i

dentitie
s.

Etherally stanced

When the

unseen wind
s took hold

of only the
top of those

tree-distan
cing moment

s The rest
seemed as if

rooted in a
perpetual

ly silenc
ed down-feel.

Slow movements *(Mozart Piano Concerti)*

slowing down

as stream
s in the sum

mertime of a
reverent

ial quiet
that touches

more the soul–
fingered

delicate
ly refined

enchant
ments.

Little per

sons in big

position
s shadowing

a longer reach
than they

could possi
bly hold.

Soul-sound

s when the

music slow
s to space–

invoking si
lences.

Madoff

Living a

life of big
country-club

impression
s that left

his users
as an empt

ied pool with
that dried–

seasoned a
wareness.

Family-sense

often in

voked with
those inward

ly touching
eyes though

only ready–
proofed if

it can stand–
up to an e

qually shar
ed inherit

ance.

Appearance

often im

plies less
than it act

ually mean
s as if cloth

ed for decept
ively self–

enhancing
s.

Friend *(à la Confucius) (for Chung)*

ship only

if we can
stand on e

qualled ground
with a chosen

width of envis
ioned self-en

lightening
s.

Rhetorically

His words

however ele
vated to the

heights of his
pulpit's self–

confining o
ratory left

him mid–air
suspended

to a vacant
ly echoing

response.

Out-dated

He plann

ed so far
ahead that

time (suspic
iously routed

on the same
track) caught

up on its
eager competi

tor heel
ed him to a

stopped–down
no–go.

Endangered

Awared to

danger that
heighten

ed feel of
only-now'

s suspic
iously off–

colored as
a hare hunt

ed in its
blood–scent

ed track
s.

For Rosemarie

Your child–

like innocen
ce (the kind

of purity
rarely seen)

as if protect
ing from a

world that
had known

too much.

"Realism"

continual

ly redefin
ing itself

the seer and
seen dialogu

ing that e
ver–closer

perspecti
ved–now.

Asides

Those scarce
ly spoken a

sides as if
whisper

ing between
the line'

s sun-sett
ing dimly

darken
ing.

"Ritter Teufel Tod" *(Dürer)*
(Knight Devil Death)

keeping

always clos
er to that

distanc
ing path

through
those wood

ed darkness
es that

could almost
be heard clos

ing him stead
ily behind.

Squirrelled

Jumped quick

er than his
landing-right

s could be
coming assur

ed of another
sending-off

tail-length
ed recurr

ing world-
finding
s.

Behind

the lines

keeping the
quiet endan

gered in an
enemied

world of
one mistake

and he'll be
found-out

covering o
ver those

tracks that
could only

be unmistaken
ably his.

For Rosemarie

The warmth-

moulding
of your flesh

ed inner si
lences kept

me always
closer-in

tuned.

Blowing

off his loco

motived steam
until his eng

ine "huffed
and puffed"

and blew some
of those se

cretly-held
scholarly o

pinions in-
to the dust

bin of his
lonesome

ly accumula
ting past.

Taking care

of her elder

ly mother
She aged in

to the sha
dowing fear

s of another
closely dark

ening time.

That self-

revealing

light on St.
Paul's Damas

cus road
shining be

yond its
own time-en

compassing
brightness.

"Making God

his partner"

in good–deed
s money–ven

tured he be
came invest

ed with that
lordly throne

higher indeed
than any o

ther form of
self–decept

ion.

Otherwise? *(Viktor Frankl)*

"And if it

was you" a
jobless Ger

man feeding
on the growth

of a young
family "would

you have done
its other

wise?"

Meant to kill

He never knew

he was meant
to kill as

if called
from the sha

dows of a
nother's reach–

grasping his
all-encompass

ing hand's
heart–down.

A familiar

road with a

strange new
feeling of

not having
been there be

fore it open
ed out into

a spacious
park soundless

ly all–aware
enclosing e

choless ac
cords.

For Rosemarie

How could

you at 73
still becom

ing the
spring-time

of my own
self-renew

al.

Number

s were for

him most al
ways anony

mously mark
ing-off of

what retain
ed some ob

scured self-
meaning Until

they brand
ed him with

a hot iron
indelibly

only-there.

Philanthro

py (however

good it may
mean) a self–

facing way
of making good

for an insat
iable money–

sense.

Timed-appearances

Diffuse

leafed–
shadow

ings on the
aging wood

of this 1938
house as if

bringing it
back to those

never–to–be–
forgotten

times through
the lush green

of its spring–
lit appear

ances.

For Rosemarie *(50ᵗʰ wedding anniversary)*

Our love

blooming
out of the

blood and
ash of those

desparate
times defying

all the rule
s of marriage

German and
Jew love-re

conciling
that irrecon

cilable past.

Wood

worms culti

vating a qual
ity taste

for the fin
est (authenti

cally proven)
time-bespoken

treed-thought
s.

The spring-

fullness of
this resurrect

ing Sunday
all greened–

aflow with
Christ's bloss

oming promise.

Ashamed

I've been

ashamed of
myself more–

than–enough
at least I

remember
where it most

hurts while I
hope others

won't re
discover

my naked
ly alone of

that dark–
down pit.

For Rosemarie

Common

lengths as
walking in

stride even
shadowing

much the
same pulse

d heart-flow
ing unity-

of-self.

Horsed-up

The few time
s against

those I clos
er-felt horsed-

up as my fa
ther's only

son left me
incredulous

ly sad-at-
heart bott

omed-down.

His own way

He alway

s went his
own way

as if the
road-signs

would in-
time adjust

to his seld
omed need

s for go
ing through.

Freed

mostly as

sail-boat
ing the wind'

s own sense-
for-direct

ing her to
a skied-open

blue.

Blood-

ties many of

us up in–
to knotted

relation
s that (how

ever tight)
rarely can

be undone.

The letter

carefully

phrased how
ever person

ally touch
ed by conceal

ing those un
der–surfaced

innuendoe
s.

Last 3 symphonies (Mozart)

so strong

ly contrapun
ctual rhyth

mically clash
ing those in

resolving dis
sonant under–

currents
Where' s the fine

ly-poetic Mo
zart (or was

it the conduct
or) almost

seemed as if
hiding him

self out.

Clara Schumann

holding-off

the young im
petuous Brahm

s knew that
(for her)

love as a
first and

always-only
as those

roses of re
membrance

on his cold–
stoned grave.

For Rosemarie

If there'
s something

of that little–
girl–left eye–

choosing
ly dressed

for the flor
id design

s of your
clothed–in

terior ap
praisal

s.

Mozart

andante's

his free–flow
ing poetic

intuition
s whereas

Haydn adagio'
s the abstract

depths of spac
ially sound–

proofed.

Who would

have thought
that Germany

could become
an island of

peaceful-tran
quility after

it had blooded
Europe down

to the rock-
bed of its

very-being
now enclosed

from a world
threatened

at all sides
Who would

have thought ...

Milkweed (2)

a) Milkweed'

s so light
that not e

ven the wind
s could de

cipher its
outlast

ing flight.

b) Milkweed'

s the white

ness of our
ever-blown

flighty i
magining

s.

May 10*th*

Israel day

with all those
flags and

speeches high–
flying the

fear of sett
ling down

half–mast.

He let

the air in

volving an o
pening–out

from all
those closed–

in darken
ing thought

s of his.

"The road not taken" (Robert Frost)

A mistaken

moment (or
was it just

her off-balan
cing percept

ions) reading
the signs

wrong that
led her that

other-way from
"the road not

taken".

Cat-like

We may need

those "sim
ple truths"

once again
A wisdom

that belittle
s the wealth

of our intri
cately unrav

elling a
ball-of-wool

cat-like.

Team-play'

s a precis

ioned–sens
ing where the

other is
Not the big

stars' outshining
their self–

importan
ces.

The ambigu

ity of lang
uage mirror

ing the where
and why–not'

s of our own
insuffic

ient cause–
sense.

Making-fun

of what

one doesn'
t under

stand any
higher-sense

of their own
as a pulpit

staired to
be coming

down-from.

I never could

imagine be

coming old
Only now I

experience
what's unimag

inably there.

That middle-

sized slender

dog sleek and
statuesque

ly posed as
a bygone Roman

emperor.

String quartet #2 *(Brahms)*

The flow

ing of heav
ily involved

voices accumu
lating their

insisting
sound–

depths.

His dream

s interwov
en into an

imagery of
long-lost

time-recall
ings.

That Brahms'

f minor piano

quintet length
ened the span

of its classi
cally confin

ing time–
sense into

a diffuse
ly over-felt

never-ending
s.

Suitability

When appear

ance dressed–
up for all

and varied oc
casions be

comes the
measure of

man's inher
ent suitabil

ity.

True-test

When daily-

living become
s the true-

test of love'
s wear-abili

ty as the de
lighting i

magery of a
Persian car

pet's worn-
down to its

foot-fading
bottomness-

loss.

Or words

learning to
occupy their

thorough
ly right

ness-accord
s.

Being-told

When tour

ing become
s being-told

what and why
to see like

listening–
up on a con

cert by read
ing the pro

gram–notes
through–I'

d rather be
programm

ed into its
seeing me

hearing me
out of my

own preferen
tial pre-ex

posures.

Authenticity

No one can

hear a work
as the compos

er intended
his other–

time placed
in the pro

cess of where
he's becoming

my listen
ing offside

but neverthe
less intent

ly so.

The wrong side

The Israel

ites favored
their king

the God-anoint
ed–Saul with

his intend
ing power–

claims over
the shepherd–

boy David flee
ing for his

life–lines

And so the

Viennese
took a let–

down on the
late Mozart

and Beethoven
favoring what'

s popular–ap
preciable –

We're most
ly on the

wrong side
of where we

shouldn'
t want

to be.

Aaron became

Moses' shadow

lengthed in
his God–voic

ing accords
But outside

of that fall
en to the

shadows of
his God–free

ing guilt.

Towers *(4)*

a) The Tower of Babylon

One almost

couldn't
measure the

height of
that build

ing contin
ually expand

ing sound
lessly be

yond its own
sense of

self–import
ance.

b) The Tower of Siloah

when it fell

killing many
asked Jesus

"Who's re
sponsible"

He answer
ed by star

ing through
the depths of

their lower
ing eyes

"All of you
repent".

c) The World Trade Building

symbol of

wealth and
achieve

ment tower
ing over a

city of a "all-
that-money

could-buy"
Now the

ground-zero
of those

scarcely de
ciphering

innocent
cries.

d) Centuries

of church-

heights as
piring to

those seclud
ed realms

of an invis
ible God

now emptied
of faith

sold off
one-by-one

to the high
est bidder.

Tennyson

may have

been contin
ually on the

look-out for
just-the-right-

themes to
match his sup

erior crafts
manship My

themes on-the-
other-hand

outlooking me
as those har

boured light
s guiding

this waved
ship-of-mine

lonesome
ly ashore.

Jonathan

as eldest

son of King
Saul his right

ful successor
ornament

ed with all
those kingly

attribute
s faith just

ice and the
power-of-the-

sword Where
as The good

Lord chose in
his stead

a multi-talent
ed adulter

er and murder
er David the

poetic sheph
erd-boy.

"Jew-boy"

he called

me danger
ously out-

of-date but
honestly-

direct for
one he'd

never seen
before.

Eichmann

changed a

gain into o
ther cloth

es (as if
he wouldn't be

standing na
ked to the

good Lord's
judgment)

No longer
Hannah Arendt'

s "banality
of evil"

but the evil
ness itself

killing for
the sake of

killing
more Jews.

Warmth

rains a

summer-spell
that season

ed our skin
dissolving

into the
touch of

their muted
echoing

s.

Remembran

ces of per

sons that
could hard

ly be brought-
to-mind as

if time had
changed place

with its van
ishing past-

sense.

As if rain

has a voice-
of-its-own

hurried at
times inward

ly repeat
ing in scar

cely deciph
ering phras

es.

"Where do we come from (Gauguin 1897)

What are we

Where are we
going" The

phases of
life color

ed through a
mysterious

sense of time
lessness.

M. K.

He held

straight-up
to what he

thought and
believed

as if the
world would

become a
truth less

without his
question

ing why.

So much

He wanted

to say some
thing so much

that he could
n't say it

right.

If every

thing become
s known as

a woman with
hard-press

ed feature
s If they'

re no secret
s left no

mysterious
ly unknown

side-street
s Then life

can run its
daily course

to our rou
tined selved–

satisfact
ions.

If poem

s redefine

what we've
always known

then life
remains

change
ably intent.

When

thought

s run in
to words

as stream
s vacant

ly alive.

For Neil

The same

place same
persons 2

years later
hardly self–

revealing
as if time

could no
longer re

cognize it
self.

If build

ings inhabit

a life of
their own

Not even
these bared

walls could
resemble

their pre
existant

loneliness
es.

When

time seem

s to settle
down as leave

s falling
through a

quiet–slowness
of their un

heard ech
oing shadow

s.

It darken

ed as a threat
ening voice

d wind-cur
rents.

Rain

drops stream

ing down the
window as

if fleeing
from an in

definable
cause.

Redon'

s flower

s so indiv
idually

voiced as if
colour had

found its
true source

here.

First-timed pleasure

Hearing
the same music

at differ
ing phases of

one's life'
s a time-

spanning dia
logue reveal

ing again
first-timed

pleasure
s.

These

time-shift

ings shadow
ed a world

change
ably real

ized.

Umberto D.

The bench
where that

old man sat
each and e

very day in
habiting what

ever thought
s that form

ed his a
ging mind

looked just
as barren and

forsaken on
that last-long

day when he
ceased to re

appear.

First im

pressions

however pre
cise fade–

from–mind
unless

stamped
with a cer

tainty of
lasting ex

pressive
ness.

"In the best possible light"

She wanted

to be seen
"in the best

possible
light" figur

ed herself
to the fin

est of dress
ed–appear

ances mirr
oring a

strange
ness from

self a vague
scarcely dis

tinct darken
ing other

wiseness.

Horses

almost pic

turesque
ly time–pos

ing sudden
ly stamped

in a vibran
cy of ech

oing sun–
downs.

Birds

sang through

the cool–dark
ness their

voiced ton
alitie's

colored.

Size in

music poetry
and art has

rarely real
ized a con

sistent
density of

tonal express
iveness.

The Gold-weigher *(2) (Vermeer)*

a) As if time

were held

still here
so spacial

ly gold–ex
acting.

b) She weigh

ed with eye
s closed to

a higher
sense of judg

ment.

She had a

way of doing

things wrong
by meaning

so well–in
volving for o

thers too
much of her

own short–
sighted

ness.

Women

who need a

man (some per
haps don't)

leave me
with an in

complete
sense of Cran

ach's Eve so
oft lessen

ed from her
ground-base.

Cranach's "Fall of man"

so varied in

its inter
change

able guilt
that even the

"apple" seem
s at times

as if taint
ed through

with an even-
more of that

always tempt
ing bite.

Cranach'

s imperfect

anatomy per
haps imply

ing more a
bout man's

nature than
the painter'

s visably
short-coming

s.

Strauss-Kahn *(2)*

as a jungl

ed tiger
looming for

prey sprang
out of the

depths of his
shadowing

self flesh
ing for taste

of a woman-
kind.

Strauss-Kahn *(DSK)*

rediscover

ing his mirr
ored face-de

ceiving fa
cades.

Cranach'

s "Adultress"

caught in
the act of a

feared-shame
Jesus soften

ed-down to
His word-with

holding their
stone-hard

preparat
ions.

The Dutch

"Golden age"

flattened–down
perspect

ives "land
scaping" oft

more clouds
than earth–

dwelling con
clusions.

Vermeer'

s painting

within paint
ings can (as

with his win
dowing scene

s) also im
ply the in

side/out of
her timed–

sensed ex
posure

s.

Imprison

ed (as he
always was)

but now a
gainst those

closed–down
instinct

s of his.

Plane-

high over

the unseen
ocean's blue–

becoming
s.

Sleep recon

ceives the

where of our
being other

wise than
now.

Ships at

sea floating

upon a depth
of untold si

lences.

At night

the curtain

s closed
down their

untoucha
ble aware

nesses.

As if flow

ers (unseen)

at first) im
plying a fra

grance of
night's allu

sive color
ings.

Scarsdale'

s a window

ed-town as
if to a voi

ced aware
ness.

His word against hers

When it be

came only
his word a

gainst her'
s echoing

a self-de
ciding inde

cipherable
truth.

After

rain even

the woods
seemed as

if quiet
ly self-re

solving.

A flag'

s really no

thing more
than a long

thin pole
striped and

starred to
a symbolic

length–of–
seeing.

Strauss-Kahn

hand–cuffed

to that fear
fully unsha

ven face of
his imply

ing a guilt
as yet unpro

ven–pre–decid
ings.

After her

husband'

s death she
became increa

singly less
of her re

motely dis
tancing

self.

Waiting

the tension

of unresol
ving pre

sence.

Her room

carefully

composed of
artificial

flowers de
prived of

the linger
ing softness

of their
scented depth–

perspect
ives.

On coming

rain–thought

s closed in
a density of

all–consum
ing green

ness.

That pom

pous apple

rounded to a
redness of

its lush–ful
filling tasti

ness.

For Rosemarie'

s little-budd

ed kiss-awak
ening my

peaked-
through lip

s those pre
forming route

s of out
spreading

sweetness
es.

Double-timed

Was it an ap

parition of
Walter so

quietly self-
containing

Suddenly
voiced as a

swan's final
song contin

uing a resum
ée of all

that hadn'
t been said

double-tim
ed.

Polonius

hiding be

hind the cur
tain from

whatever
truth's be

yond the
grasp of that

deadly-blood
ed dagger.

This room

(the poet'
s) secrect

ly confid
ing an un

spoken less
er-sense-of-

self.

Fresh

winds cool

ing the im
pression

s of skin-
light aware

nesses.

With her

eyes accust

omed to a
routine of

view not e
ven the ex

pansing tree
s could rise

above her li
mited hori

zoned-length.

Echoed

It was those

long-extend
ing hallway

s darken
ing from view

that echoed
more of his

own continu
ous shadow

ings.

He knew

that was the

question
she wouldn'

t answer dark
ly conceal

ing the depth
s of her hidd

en memorie
s.

The long

ing–sadness

of Stephen
Foster's song

s left him
with that

homeless
feeling of

not knowing
where.

Facts and fancies

Those used

to a world
so firm and

fit shadow
lessly self–

confining
a no–ways–

out.

Soft sum

mer winds as

if whisper
ing through

those un
heard silen

ces of their
s.

Dream-

like city

distanc
ing from be

ing heard as
if time had

left it there
creating

soundless
remembran

ces.

The slow

procession

al flow of
clouds as if

called to an
unspoken bey

ondness.

Realmed *(2)*

a) A house

roomed so

spacious
ly alive

that it
realmed its

own sense–
of-being.

b) Why the ri

ver winding–

its–own–way
through the

earth's out
spreading e

ven beyond
the realm

s of its
self-becom

ings.

Beds hard

ly ever used

pleasant
ly surface-

decorating
a sense of

prim-flower
ed self-re

vealings.

An uninhab

ited house al
most self-suf

ficiently
standing to

some abandon
ed purpose

of-its-own.

As a small

silent lake

calming our
own self-re

flecting
wave-length

s.

The self-suf

ficient turtle
housed and ar

moured to the
steadied pace

of its foot-
nearing time-

seclusion
s.

Time stopp

ed a silence

spreading
into a depth

of stilled-a
waiting color

s hesitant
ly speak

ing aloud.

The true life'

s not what'

s lived but
in the shadow

ed reflect
ions of those

lost but hesi
tantly awaken

ing moment
s.

He became

so much him

self all of
a bustle

that there
was little–

left to go a
round.

Stephen Foster'

s "Old Kentucky

home" wasn't
his but be

came more than
even–so

longing for
what was den

ied but still
inbecoming.

"Beautiful dreamer" (Stephen Foster)

"Beautiful

dreamer'
s" angeli

cally stream
ing invisi

ble heaven
ly accord

s.

Eye-seeming

an untouch

ed–asking
the soul–

length's si
lent respon

se.

Even at

the airport

the skies
seemed diff

erently ex
posing a view

of cloud–in
creasing

s.

Our sense-of-seeing

Does the wea

ther change
our sense–of–

seeing And if
not what hasn'

t been's real
izing us

back.

For George

on another

cause but his
instinct for

gain moved
him on my

parallel-track
s.

After

seeing's

though fa
ding from

sensed-re
flection

s.

Over-spaced

They were

so palaced
over-spaced

that their
shadows bare

ly held-for-
two.

Buying-back

One just

can't buy–
back the love

less time
s that left

such a pit
ful gap bet

ween them.

"The brown" ... *(Bardstown, Kentucky)*

a stylish

hotel that
left (even

me) hungry
for a finish

ing noun just
looking at...

Sparring

may be just

an animal
way of lock

ing horns
But some can

gore the
guts out of

one's prevail
ing good-in

tention
s.

Stephen Foster'

s oft-timed

yearning
for place

s he'd never
seen (a

home) early
lost that

left him
(at the end)

homeless
ly alone.

Early

summer morn

ing when man'
s asleep

and all's
still peopl

ed with a si
lent almost

untoucha
ble purity.

Haydn's Creation (5)

a) When only

space create

s the realm
of an almost

timeless-
tensioned

to His light–
fulfill

ing breath.

b) The worm

left me

bottomed-
down to the

length of
its increas

ingly life-
impulsing

s.

c) Music

(then) is

not sound
but light–

incausing
the life of

where sound
emerges

spaceful
ly attuned.

d) Those lov

ing doves
repeated

ly encirc
ling the

not-enough
of their

caressing
ly appeal

s.

e) When God

remained

voiceful
ly attuned

even beyond
man's self–

ennobling
fall.

Flower

s looked

on too long
staid and

shallow Or
was it their

seclusive
response

to his off de
clining

eye–span.

Sun-sett

ing harmon

ies refin
ing the flow

ered expanse
of time's

withhold
ing express

iveness.

For Rosemarie

An aging to

getherness
as words

that coalesce
to a common

phrasing.

The two-of-them

I couldn'

t get behind
the two-of–

them indepen
dent and yet

common bor
dered to a

where of my
no-finding–

out.

Mirandolina (5) (*Goldoni*)

a) "I am who I am"

the Marquis

(almost penni
less) exalt

ing his low
ly state

with the ele
vating height

of a noble
man's name–

claims But
(as Shakes

peare re
minds us)

"What's in
a name".

b) "I am who I am"

as if an aris

tocratic title
could shield

the Marquis
from his true–

state–of–be
ing imperson

ed only in
appearan

ces as those
actresses

staging whom
they really

aren't.

c)The Count

must learn

that money
and gifts

(their shiny
appearance

s) can't e
ven realize

the image of
true–love.

d) Mirandolina

(as Jane Aust

in's Emma)
plays with

the feeling
s of other

s as a mean
s of hiding

from her own.

e) The Knight

(as a woman–
hater)

can't really
hate what

he's never
known hiding

(as the o
thers) be

hind a fa
cade of self–

protection.

He could

survive

those aging
symptoms of

use as long
as the end'

s recreat
ing the start

of a new be
ginning.

Re-forming

We all real

ize our un
known source

s re-form
ing their sha

dowing state
in-to the ex

plicit ex
pressive

ness of
our own.

"That suffering artist"

That romant

ic image of
"the suffer

ing artist"
often for

gets those
real depths

of an all-in
volving dark

ness sensed
deeply with

in those untold
realms of

our all-encom
passing self.

His facial

prettiness
as a cherub

classical
ly choiring

without an
apparent

message to
be darkly

spent.

So much to say

He had so

much to say
that the say

ing it left
him near-empt

ied voiceless
ly aloned.

For Rosemarie

The fullness

of this last
ing summer

those love-
immersing

days brought
to fruition

a complete
ness of our

scarcely
wanting-for-

more.

The fear of loss

    (however much
    we've been

    given) the
    biblical 5

    talents to
    be spent for

    the all–invok
    ing sake of

    Him.

Haydn

    lost the love–

    of–his–life
    to a God re

    plentish
    ing with the

    fullness
    of a gift

    ed otherwise
    ness.

The play

fully reali

zing the more
of our own

acting–out
the conscien

ce of what
we hardly

knew (but
then) express

ively reveal
ing.

Each morning

collecting

those dead
(almost weight

less) bees
strangely

felt from an
(as yet)

undefining
source.

Overcast

the close

ly-within-
feeling of

almost breath
lessly un

touched.

"It was his

word against

hers) as if
words could de

cide the truth
of their be

coming inex
plicitly

two-sided.

"Making up for lost time"

as if time

could become
unlost by

its present
ly rediscov

ering.

A poet

can make

one aware
of what was

scarcely
known so pre

cisely as
if it was al

ways so.

"Wild strawberries" (Ingmar Bergman)

became the

endless
ly receding

woods envel
oping more of

him than
could have

been reali
zing why.

Lovely Rose

marie's blond
curls pillow

ed-asleep of
dreams encom

passing her
timeless

ly beyond.

This morn

ing motion

lessly held
as if time

itself had
been stilled

overspread
ing.

Your way

If you can

help people
to seeing

it your way
may not be

so aloned
as before.

Street

>lights still
>
>becoming
>the appear
>
>ance of morn
>ing's stead
>
>ily growth.

She didn't

>try at it
>became the
>
>more of
>what she
>
>wasn't.

Self-satis

>fied's state-
>
>of-being stat
>ued out-timed
>
>beyond its
>always hav
>
>ing been
>arrived.

Tobey' *(1963 owned by the poet)*

s dance–

like rhythm
ically

touched-a
live its own

echoing'
s called.

The moon'

s night–har

vesting its
(almost) mag

netic glow.

What it is

as the spid

er netted
to its art

istically
interwov

en need
for taste.

False start

whistled

back to that
over-drawn

starting
line's end–

of-a-beginn
ing.

Does the use

of language

mirror (per
haps only

scarcely re
fining) those

inner accord
s of self

Or does it
reflect what

education
should have

left its
touched-sens

ings behind.

Poems from Berlin *(13)*

a) The city'

s silent

only the
sleepless

windows
as if faced

from stone.

b) (Vermeer)

The woman
seduced by

music and
wine face

lessly appar
ent (the

proof's
tabled–on

display).

c) DeHooch

at the oppos

ite end from
Vermeer with

its light my
sterious

ly leading
out that

room spac
iously–per

soned even be
yond the domes

tic height
of that wo

man's outer
reach.

d) Master from Flémalle'

s portrait

of a prefig
uring fat

man's face
puckered

to his cheek'
s insolent

ly self–sus
taining.

e) Geertgen Tot

Sint Jan'
s St. John

the Baptist
dreamily

landscap
ing the fold

s of his
through-spell

ing reverie
s.

f) Altdorfer'

s Birth of

Christ tid
ily hidden

in the future
remains of

the temple
s he'd re

place through
the blood

and tears of
his lasting

redemption.

g) Cranach'

s Fall of Man

with Adam
and Eve em

bracing that
together

ness–fruit
but Eve's

feet out–pos
itioned from

their natur
al stance.

h) Rembrandt'

s Man of Sorrow

s thinned–down
to that wood–

enhancing
length for

feared–hold
ings.

i) Petrus Christus'

Annunciation

a seldom
naïve-fine

ness of touch
ed–flowing

hair and
cloth close

ly chosen
to that e

ternal mo
ment of vir

ginal flower
ing.

j) Memling'

s Mary and

Child the
apple as the

fruit of
man's fall

held by The
Virgin to

Christ's
grasping in

stinct for
the futur

ing claim
s.

k) Memorial

for the dead

Jews samed
as they were

to a name
lessly ston

ed–in si
lence.

l) Berlin'

s prominent

impression
of a city

with a bur
ied past

reborn to
its almost

proudly self–
securing.

m) Pre-involving

At a height

bird–perched
over the city

left him spac
iously pre–

involving.

One couldn'

t look at

her strange
ly gestured

nervous word
s that couldn'

t find their
own sense

of being here
and only her

s.

Berlin'

s a home

less city re
claiming

what it's
trying to

forget a marr
iage of two

parts that
can't quite

become e
qualled to

a common one
ness.

"The rest was silence" *(Shakespeare)*

When a marr

iage's done
and gone that

neither end
could meet a

gain at the
center a

speechless
void that "the

rest was si
lence".

Familied

How can "a

new family"
of the faith

ful survive
intact when

the old one
familiar

ied through
blood and

birth's sel
dom retain

ing its cer
tained grasp-

on–us.

Berlin

the most anon

ymous of cit
ies with a

history chill
ing one's

blood down
to its most

existen
tial heart-

beat.

Berlin

If cities

could see and
hear this

one (so modern
ly self-assum

ing) would
turn its face

away ashamed
to realize

the darkness
of its still

all-consum
ing past.

"Life must go on"

but for the

millions
then there

was no going
on subsumed

to blood and
the ash of

an unremem
bering past.

Words

The "Dick

and Jane" of
my 1ˢᵗ grade

past left me
staring at

words (how
ever clear

ly spelled–
out) that

couldn't pa
per Dick and

Jane really
alive.

Even God i

magined be

fore He spoke
in picture

s that color
ed me alive

to Dick and
Jane's life–

being.

The Frogs *(Aristophanes) (2)*

a) These ones

not very much
for jumping a

bout though
as the biblic

al frogs invad
ing private

sources leaf–
sitting spec

ulations
Here on Euri

pedes and Aesch
uylos as if

literary crit
ique could

replace the un
derlying ten

sions of drama
tic art.

b) There's a

time of no–
turning-back

What's no long
er believed

can't be re
trieved even

the rhetoric
of Aeschuylos

expresses
those strik

ing accords of
his faith dy

ing as the
Athens of your

irretrieva
ble times.

On the outside

We've often

seen them
there on the

outside div
ided from

that sacred
scene by a

fence a wall
but more so

by their cur
ious-intent

for not
realizing

why.

What next

where next

this world as
a boat cast-

off from its
moorings in

to the sea
of change

able tides
out-harbour

ed from its
place of no

return.

Bombed-out

to the very–

depth of
their conscious

less self–stri
vings only to

be rebuilt
from those in

visible ash
ened remain

s.

The route

they'd taken

as those
long lines of

the disposs
essed grow

ing daily to
the wave–like

immensity
of a return

ing where
they'd never

arrived.

2nd *Commandment* (Moses)

They creat

ed God in the
image of their

own desiring
need for love

forgiveness
and the grace

of sacred hour
s But He stood

outside their
self-embell

ishing claim
s in the

dwelling in
darkness

of His own un
touchable do

main.

Parentless

Born he was

into a parent
less future

alone even
before he had

come to real
ize the depth

of that all–
encompass

ing seclus
ion.

At the end

without e

ver turning
back Each

looked to
save (if noth

ing more than
himself) from

Sodom's relent
lessly salt–colum

ned flame
s.

Excuse

    s oft–become

    a hide–and–
    seek from one'

    s own shadow
    ing claim

    s.

András Schiff's Variation recital
(Munich, June 7) (4)

    a) Sonata op. 111

    (Beethoven slow mvt.)

    almost im

    pression
    istically

    spacing (self-
    sounding)

    an inner re
    solved–final

    ity of god
    ful reconcil

    iation.

*b) F minor Varia
tions (Haydn)*

The never–a

ging–Haydn al
most fateful

ly redesign
ing his youth

ful romantic
exposure

s.

*c) Schumann's "Ghostly
Variation'*

s" as if Mendels
sohn dream

ily guiding
him through

those unexplor
ed realms of

Hades' death–
invoking

calls.

d) Variations sérieuses
(Mendelssohn)

That theme

took ahold
on his form

ing its
self–emerg

ing sound–
lengths.

It rained

an envelop

ing darkness
down to the

interiors of
where silence

reigned supre
mely self–sus

taining.

Suspicion

breeds a dis

coloring
blood contag

iously a
ware.

That disease

hidden from

its unknown
source stead

ily growing in
to the depth

ed-soul of
our gardened i

magination.

Those men

(however bright

and self-dis
ciplined)

who (animal-
like) can't

deny their in
stinctual

need for wo
men's softly

enticing
flesh.

Art therapy

When art be

comes the ser
vant of a

("higher") per
sonal cause

used out be
cause it can'

t create a
beauty of all–

its–own–kind.

This heavy

hanging–down

kind of day
as the weight

of being clos
ed–in the

brooding depth
of one's own

solemn self–
immersing

thought
s.

A sanctified realm

When love'

s not accord
ed a sancti

fied realm of
its own as

those untouch
ed silence

s that speak
because they'

re so long
in being list

ening for.

Jewelry

(as she sens

ed) might
embellish

that shining–
up smile of

hers.

That fruit

(hardly dis

tinguish
able at

first) a
midst a plea

surable gar
den of time

ly pursuits
ripened to

the full–flow
of its eye–

tempting ex
posure

s.

He experien

ced so much

of an inter
ior kind

that he could
hardly remem

ber the this
or that of

why words
forming a

sparkling
brooch of

semi–precious
stones.

Clarinet Quintet *(Brahms)*

Brahms not

grandiose-
romantic

but swept-
through with

the lyrical
accords of

what over
came the depth

s of his very-
being formed.

Brahms

at his best

in the deep
ly colored

richness
of darkly re

sounding in
terior tonali

ties.

The image

of the young–

sensitive
Brahms pian

istical
ly pleasing

brothel–in
tending sail

ors with only
the poetry of

Eichendorff
and Heine

still–hold
ing most of

his express
ive aware

ness.

"Beethoven's 5th Symphony
for flute and piano"

Rearrang

ing what the
composer and o

therwise arti
culately de

fined to his
own aesthet

ic needs im
plies "we can

do it better"
Or just most

ly "innocent
ly" expanding

a limited in
strumental

repertoire.

These time-

shifting

clouds heav
ily deepen

ing the mo
mentary ton

alities of
our own in

terior cause
s.

Rained out

These contin

uous days-of-
rain left

him realiz
ing the need

of his be
ing so rain

ed-out from
those deepen

ing darkness
es within.

White bloss

oms in a
dark time

of day as if
jewelled to

a hardly-known
awareness

scarcely re
mote.

Otherwise

as when

dreams create
their own

sense of time
and place un

easily other
wise.

Eichendorff

realized

those dark
quietude

s of a wood
ed density

moon-alight.

For Rosemarie

As I redis

covered my
Jewishness

through Christ'
s suffering

s So have I
realized

that fullness
of self-trans

scending
the oneness-

of-us.

Out-of-line

He stepped

out-of-line
denying

their ever-
present rhy

thmic cause
into an in

describ
able vast

ness of un
rehearsed

beginning
s.

Brahms

created a

richness
of sound as

the fulfill
ed summer-

growth to
its density

of green
ness.

What if

they didn'

t take of
that forbidd

en fruit
would still

have ripen
ed to its

all-intend
ing fall?

They warn

ed him not

to step be
yond that in

visible line
that kept

drawing him
there ever-

closer.

Do birds

listen to

those samed
tonalitie

s of their
always-re

peating voice
And if they

did chang
ing its uni

quely rhythm
ic coloring

s.

A true dia

logue implie

s that what'
s remember

ed in alter
nating pattern

s richly self-
assuming.

Poetry

word-precis

ing what will
always re

main elusive
ly untold.

It's those

intelling

truths of
vaguely self–

revealing a
world that'

s expanding
even beyond

the limits
of it's real

izing where.

Thereness

He became so

afraid of wo
men (or of

his blemish
ed instinct

s for more)
than he could

resolve to a
quieting

source of
self–inhabit

ing there
ness.

When

ever she

turned those
dining-room

lights on
to an aware

ness of sil
ver-light's de

claring.

Thought

s without

becoming in
toned to

their intrin
sic image-ap

pearing as
statues to

the mind
less touch

ings of wind.

These tree

s sounding

out cloud–
forming an

expanse of
heavenly

spacial at
tunement

s.

The trout (Schubert)

innocent

ly gracing
the water

s with its
light-rhythm

ic inter
ludes.

Wind-

stilling

these patt
erns of leave

s a mosaic
of time-re

calling
dream-

lights.

Chamber music

at its best

an intimacy
of through-

spoken self-
realiz

ing accord
s.

A poem'

s more like

a fish-on-
the-line

pulling
tightly its

own way But
then called-

into its
self-retriev

ing fineness
es.

For Rosemarie

even after

49 years a
familiar

together
ness contin

ues to re
create its

own select
ively–inher

ent life–
finds.

Nowheres but *(3)*

a) The cat

pulling on

a ball–of–
wool unravel

ling the in
tricacie

s of its no
wheres–but–

now.

b) Preaching

only if that

finger's be
ing pointed

(as Caravagg
io's Calling

of St. Matt
hew)

at a nowhere
s-but-him.

c) Addicted

The slot–

machine
lighten

ing his ex
ploring

eyes to a
nowheres–

but-now.

Even as a

child he

knew of an
enemy out to

get him hidd
en in that

somewhere
s of not–find

ing out until
that late–au

tumn day he
caught up on

him trailing
his own foot

steps until
they stopped–

dead in a for
bidden wood'

s echoing
his own

sound
less thought

s.

Enmeshed

Those philo

sophical cat
egories left

him enmeshed
in the nets

of where e
ven Schubert'

s trout lamed
and desolate

ly forsaken
from its free-

flowing need
for the pur

ifying wa
ters of those

boundless
ly unimpair

ed light-ex
posures.

Her own way

She went

her own way
in need of

no-other-help
than finding

her own All
smiles and ap

parent concern
s for the well-

being of o
thers.

Time was runn

ing out on

her as quick
ly passed

as the sil
ver-shine

of a stream
summer-dried

from its self-
pursuing rhy

thmic accord
s.

"Facing up"

to oneself

as if that
mirrored

smile of her
s stopped ans

wering back
blankly self-

deluding.

Two-way street

That ambigu

ity of lang
uage open

ing out a two–
way street

travelling
both–at–once

most assured
ly self–apprai

sing oppos
itely direct

ioned.

What could

have been

isn't mapped–
out anymore

except in
that dream–

light of self–
eluding ex

posures.

3 poems on poem *(for Warren)*

a) How it's

said chang

es the true
measure

of its oft–
repeated

meaning
s.

b) If the poem'

s "too per

fect to be
true" Then

"truth" may
need another

measure
of its imper

fectly de
signed.

c) If other

voices mingle

in the pulse
of my own

setting course
I still de

clare the flag
s free for

their own
wind–ensuring

message
d–coloring

s.

Last stop

in the mid

st of the
woods the

train stopp
ed where it

never did be
fore he could

find the where
of being the

only one left
tightly con

cealed from a
no–ways–out.

Tiny eye-

    dots of that

    darkly-assem
    bling bird'

    s touch-of-
    an-after

    thought's
    only in flight

    becoming
    the where of

    where it
    really wasn'

    t.

The wind

    s invisib

    ly there
    revealing

    the touch of
    a coolness

    momentar
    ily breathed-a

    wakening
    s.

A friend

ship (their

s) as two
boats sail

ing their
own separate

ways but still
(years–long)

returning
to their oft

abandoned
(but still

chosen)
port.

His wife

(in a free–

finding marr
iage) pursu

ing her own
self–endear

ing course
While he (as

a complacent
dog) leashed

on to her
footsteps

following.

A family

less self-e

mancipat
ing society

is like arti
ficial flower

s rained and
sunned for

their earth
less growth.

An umbrell

ared world

in these rain-
downed time

s of multi
colored pro

tective in
stincts

shadow-en
closing those

forward-lean
ing steps

of ours.

Boredom

at the heart

of nothing
spaceless

ly time-con
suming.

Poemed *(for Warren)*

If a poem

isn't length
ed to its

pre-determin
ing form

If it derive
s more word

ly-alive than
its meaning

s could poss
ibly hold

If the spac
ing of its

becoming
known doesn'

t reveal the
more of its

only now that
poem isn't

really poem
ed-at-all.

Their eye

s magneti

cally hold
ing those

spell–bound
silence

s.

"To make sure"

They just

wanted "to–
make–sure"

as if life
could only

be certain
ed of–any

thing–else
than its own

unsuret
ies.

That other self

He wrote him

self into
that other

self secret
ly enclosed

from its own
withhold

ing power
s of mean

ing.

When flower

ing colors
blend into

the immutab
le sounds of

these retell
ing wind's

phrasing
alike.

Summer how

ever bright

ly intuned'
s a length–

of–seeing e
ven beyond

the scope of
those vast

ly reclin
ing thought

s of his.

Is this

change

able weath
er mirror

ing the ons
and offs of

these unstead
ied times

as a compass
holding-fast

to its un
known destin

ation.

a) Illmensee

the lake so

intimate
ly small as

if voiced
with an en

closing sense
of scarce

ly reveal
ing thought

s.

b) The lake

mirror

ing shadow
s inexpli

citly formed
as moment

s hardly
heard retreat

ing into
the winds of

time's voice
less past.

c) Lilies

of the lake

cultivat
ing colors

of these wave–
retreating

sensed–impres
sions.

d) Speaking

big as if

his authori
tative voice

could over–
tone the im

pending
thoughts of

others.

e) The grass

freshly cut

to the slop
ing design

s of its in
trinsic co

lorings.

g) Can these

waters sleep

when the wind'
s aflow with

dreamed–re
veries of a

long–forgott
en past.

The wind

s (however

remotely
sourced)

visibly-
felt while

touching
the distan

ces they had
left so va

cantly be
hind.

Alena'

s rabbit-

drawing with
those thank

fully carrot-
speaking ear

s innocent
ly self-pro

tecting a
gainst the

instinct
ive predator'

s awareness-
finds.

If there'

    s nothing

    left to be
    loved except

    appearance-
    sake surfac

    ing (as Pi
    casso's draw

    ings) an emp
    tiness-at–

    heart.

Green rain

    s wind-sound

    ing alarms
    of those

    restless
    ly inhabit

    ing fear
    s.

She couldn'

    t be held

    back from
    saying what

    she knew
    wouldn't help

the saying–it
swelling to

its own voic
ed–command

ing priorit
ies.

No one here

"I don't see

a soul" as
if souls in

visibly in
habiting

some unknown
untouchable

sphere of
their own.

Church

bells sil

ver–sensed
brightly

sounding a
Sunday morn

ing's Christ–
ascending

s.

When Mozart

seems so wide-

eyed innocent
ly child-like

marching
his tin sold

iers harmless
ly self-attun

ed.

Papageno'

s multi-col

ored sing-
birds caged

in his own
fly-away

simplici
ties.

The winds

blew all-

his-thought
s away and

left him
(empty-voic

ed) be
hind.

Evening

colors sub
duing silen

ces a world
in watching

moon–intens
ed.

Sonnenhalde 2

Their house
and garden geo

metrically
stylized a

sterile un
ity of glass–

through per
spective

s.

After the

storm a

wind–still
that left

these through–
spoken tree

s silent
ly reflect

ive.

An old

inn roomed

with the un
heard se

crets of a
time long–

since expir
ing there.

A lone fly

glassed–in

the window
ed light of

its immov
able self–

contemplat
ions.

Out-felt

What he

shouldn'
t have said

in a moment
of truth–un

veiling its
protective

façade left
him naked

ly out–felt.

Image-end

idea as if

words could
reclaim the

mind's unseen
interior

resolve.

Dangl

ing prepos

itions as
if the truth

of those un
spoken word

s timeless
ly suspend

ing.

The wood

s creating

a density
of sound

less thought
s increas

ingly dark
ening.

Poem

ing this

world back
to a tenta

tively with
holding un

ity of sound–
presence.

Childhood

remembran

ces realiz
ing then or

through the
now of a dis

tancing per
spective.

"I've seen

it all be
fore" as if

seeing had be
come nothing

more than
your own hab

itually dull
ed–sameness

of person.

Lowering

the curtain

s down to
her self-re

vealing sha
dowing i

mage.

The morn

ing hadn't

yet risen a
bove the

brooding
depth of its

nightly ex
piring shad

ows.

For Rosemarie

You softly

lighten the
depth of my

darkening
world with

your trans
forming touch

ed–through
quietude

s.

The read

ing world and

the real world
two separate

worlds of
realizing

a unity
of response.

In flight to Dallas

The mass of

clouds mot
ionlessly

just sitting
there self–

satisfied
as a retired

professor re–
reading the

full length of
his most–orig

inal book–
finds.

Her face

cut-through

with crude
feature

s as if she'
d been slaved

and robbed
of all human

sympathy.

The poetry

of flight

time-escap
ing where the

winds have
been sourced

from their
realming

blueness
es.

Landscaped

Has man

been so land
scaped con

forming to
the interior

contours of
his self–de

signing fac
ial distinct

ions.

If he saw

it different

as a stone re
vealing the

facets of
one's hand'

s self–touch

ing apprais
als.

Stephen Foster

I may have

misspelled
his name but

I didn't
miss the spell

of his music
enchanting

a far–away
and long–last

ing past.

Dallas in summer (23)

a) It was too

hot to real
ize why

Dallas in
summer a

world of air–
condition

ed the in
side/outs

of not real
ly being

there.

b) He lean

and thought
ful as a

bean–stick
ing to a

closeted
kind of mo

dest shadow
ings.

c) Self-inhabited

The cold

sound of
these con

crete build
ings look

ing through
glass inhabi

ting him.

d) His was

a sneaky

kind of hu
mor that

left the
need for put

ting one's
own head a–

straight.

e) So many

thoughts as
shifting cloud

s overcom
ing him speech

lessly.

f) Bare wall'

s soundless
distance

s echoing
the length

of his word
less unresol

ve.

g) Night-light

s glass–

silences in
habiting

the lonely
ness of his

very–fear
s.

h) Glass re

flection

s even the
window's

silent reach
as unheard

as the lone
liness of

distant star
s.

i) Hotel room

even the warm

th-touch of
caring hand

s couldn'
t awaken it

alive from
its artifi

cially claim
ing presen

ce.

j) This schrub

bed-down land
scape dried

to those
earth-sound

s Indians
heard-once

close to
their ground-

forming in
stincts.

k) More perfor

mance than

person she
breathed

fire in her
voice-dress

ed to a path
os over-ton

ing the truth
of her every-

word.

l) Apartheid

He came out

of his humili
ating black

lower-level
less-than-

human-dignity
caged in a fear

and shame
lessly up

righted now.

m) Shadow

s on the

wall brush
ing the moon

aside from
its elusive

light–illus
ions.

n) Semi-arid

trees with

that desert-
look of i

solating
self–assert

ions.

o) Storm in-

coming

trees rest
lessly tremb

ling fears
of losing

their unity-
of–phrase.

p) Sleep

less night

s as if
time had

been routed
to another

cause than
his thought–

images could
readily con

fine.

q) In praise of Viktor Frankl

Every minute

can attain
a value of

its own as
if time were

wound–up a
new for each

and every per
sonally

self–encom
passing.

r) These thin

ly-fine bush

es wind–flow
ered from

the birth
of self-en

ticing dream
s.

s) If there was

an outside

(hot beyond
relief)

It was only
through

the glass–ex
posure so

clean that
even a bird

could break
its beak dis

covering
that inside–

out divide.

t) The harp

may be touch

ing sphere
s of angel

ic accords
but it be

came more
an instru

ment of col
oring–

through
those sen

sual earthy
pleasure

s.

u) Small and

fragile close

ly-felt leav
es held–

tight to
their branch

ed–in aware
nesses.

v) Perhaps

these semi–
arid winds

(timeless
ly repeat

ing themsel
ves) could

still hear
those Indian

callings close–
to-the-earth'

s down-sound
ing death-in

habiting
s.

w) German-Jew

ish street–

names as In
dian recall

ing-places
here a remem

brance of
what isn't

anymore
written-down

the way one
does indelib

ly-articul
ate on tomb–

stones.

Mapped-down

Europe'

s become a
map of our

Jewish suffer
ing seen

from the
height of

the plane
it doesn't

seem much-to-
matter now

as if that-
then hasn't

become a
part even of

the height
s of our

now-sensed.

Until then

I've never

been compar
ed to some

one's grand
mother (until

then) Charles
town South Caro

lina he asked
if I'd ever

been there –
All the fa

cial feature
s seemed

to fit just
fine.

Out-finding

They may

have thought
him insensi

tive for not
reacting to

words he didn'
t hear as

if words
could never

theless find
themselve

s out.

Postscript

All those i

solating
high-rises

couldn't
free Dallas

from that de
sert-feeling

of something
missing

(bared and
vacantly)

from its un
telling

past.

Slowing down *(for Chung)*

He was slow

ing down e
ven his voice

sensed for a
length of mean

ing as if think
ing out what

was feeling
in as wave

s reaching
for shore e

asing into
a sand–depth

ed slowly
carefully.

Hurry

ing bird
its color

s almost
left be

hind my mind
awake dar

ing for that
momentary

flight.

Summer

leaves cele
brating a

sense–mosaic
of choric

light–aware
nesses.

Elegy for M. W.

She died

a child–like
reverence

for some un
touchable

instinct
almost light–

assuming.

Only

if we can

feel a dog'
s pawing–

needs for af
fection can

we realize
those deeper

bonds of be
coming human.

That more-of-him

An animal'

s shameful
ly brood

ing his death–
instinct

ually inhab
iting that

more-of-him.

That more-of-us

We can only

comfort not
by words

(as we've
been taught

to believe)
But by sim

ply being
there that

more-of-us.

From books

She learn

ed more from
books than

from person
s could em

barrass her
being ashamed

at being de
pendent on

what wasn't
only paper

ing finds.

Fugue Shostakovich *(Piano Quintet)*

with some of

those implor
ingly dark-in

tonations of
Ravel's Passa

caglia moving
through the

registers of
his depth-de

scending under
ground soul.

Those apart

ments across–

the–way were
looking me

up to the
height of

where I could
only find a

windowed
self–reflect

ion.

"Uncle Tom"

may (in time)
have changed

meanings (e
ven the lang

uage of its
dated sentimen

tality) while
still remain

ing the same
inhabitant

of his epoch–
enduring im

portance.

Cobbled

city street

s leaving the
impression

of words e
choing just

faintly a re
minder of

some self-ob
scuring former

resolve.

"Sky-high"

They called

it "sky-high"
as if the

sky could be
measured

to the length
of their eye-

imagining
s.

Subdued

twilight-color

ing flower
s withhold

ing their
sense of bree

zed-through
touched-si

lences.

The heaven

s so heavy

with the depth
of our own

weighted
thoughts

loosed these
densely green

ed-impend
ing rains

fully-down
upon us.

"Out-of-hand"

That poem

got "out-of-
hand" that

it couldn't
be tighten

ed-in the
veined-grasp

ing control
suspend

ing moment
arily.

Incomplete

may belie a

nother sense-
of-complet

ion as with
Schubert'

s famed fully-
realized mis

named sympho
ny of-that-

kind.

Bruckner'

s 9ᵗʰ (per

haps weary
of Beethoven'

s) ended with
a movement

slowed to its
eternally

contemplat
ing.

Is an artist'

s sense-of-

form mirror
ing his self-

resolving tem
perament Or

does it strive
to define a

gainst his
own being o

therwise.

The ambigui

ty of lang
uage spaces a

distance be
tween our

own other-
sides-from-be

ing.

The nothing

ness of sim

ply being
there an old

man's leisure
without

thought of do
ing but only

being what
ever it was

perhaps the
shadows on

the wall's self-
reflecting.

After those

hard rains

incessant
ly rhythmed

that time–
beating pause

of an almost
gracious

sun phasing
a new sense

of light–re
vealing.

The city

cleansed

in snow so
deeply that noth

ing moved
only the sha

dows of birds'
time–encir

cling.

Lost

A way out

(he needed
that) from

all sides al
ways back to

the middle
of a labyrin

th that he
couldn't re

find his own
sense-from-

being.

What had-to-be-done

He knew what

had-to-be-
done But when

the time came
It wasn't as

it should
have been

Left him
there speech

lessly un
eased.

On "Self-Reliance" *(Emerson)*

He learned

to rely on
himself

These were
the times

when no one
else could

be trusted
He kept that

in mind as
a cashier

sorting out
the monies

into their
pre-assuming

places His
was here and

now shadow
ing as a

lone tree
a vacant

ly forgott
en land

scape.

This sky'

s been i

magining
my dreams

spreading
across the

wind's ether
eal silen

ces.

This river

conforms e

ven less than
us to those

straight-a
bout ways

it denies
while land

scaping an
alternate

(if pre-de
signing

route)
d from an

unknown
(though self-

revealing)
source.

"Knight Devil Death" *(Dürer)*

It may be

so that some
Christian

s learn more
from The Word

than from
life itself

directing
their ways

as Dürer's
"Knight Devil

Death" through
a wooded-den

sity of ever-
looming dan

gers.

That higher cause

Most women

don't main
ly appear the

way they do
dressed in

the desires
of men But as

a way of re
freshing

ly redefin
ing themselve

s mirrored
to that high

er cause of
self-appealing

thereness.

The poem

is a gift

that must be
godly-kept

as a chalice
of wine puri

fying its in
tent and as

chaste as the
touched-cool

ness of those
surrounding

flowers.

Shostakovich'

s themes

oft out-bal
ance a curved–

roundness
of dancing

expressive
ly rhythm

ic solitude
s.

A people

that prefer

s Mozart to
Beethoven'

s no longer
dangerous

heroically
self-inspir

ed drifting
into a

decaydence
without a

cause to de
fend itself

for.

Those transit

ional phase
s-of-life

(often se
cretly less–

apparent)
leave us with

out realiz
ing the where

or why of
their inde

cisive claim
s.

Weather-mood

s clouded

from appear
ance can cast

their shadow
s even deep

er than our
assumed bright

ness-of-per
son.

Retire

ment from

"life" (no
work–hours

left) him
with those ac

cumulating
emptied spac

es timeless
ly unresolv

ing.

Anticipat

ing what

would never
happen left

him tense
ly–aware of

his own sha
dowing depth.

When Baude

laire's bore

dom becomes a
relinguish

ing power
from one's own

density of
life–appeal

s.

When

words can

scarcely real
ize the ex

actness of
their intent

ly–aimed (as
a dart) with

out peripher
al enclos

ures.

Tersteegen' *(for Thomas Baumann)*

s mystical

ly freed–for–
Christ left

the full-blood
edness of my

own life-ap
peals paling.

Tagore'

s beautify

ing life's
daily allure

s expressed
transpar

ently through
its residue

s of poetic
cliché

s.

Herzogenberg'

s chamber-

works like
ably familiar

as if it's-
all-been-said-

before nice
ably ap

pealing.

From the i

mage to the
idea's trans

forming i
mage All a

"natural
process" as

of clouds in
creasing

ly self-in
volving.

When

her husband

died the
house became

larger It
spaced out

the places
where he had

left echoes
(perhaps)

but a void-
sense of long

ing vacan
cies.

Carl Stamitz'

s' little

known Viola
Concerto in

D with its
melancholy

slow movement
in D minor

so sadly in
timately

contempla
tive as if

Mozart was be
ing over

heard here.

That last move

ment (Stamitz)
attuned take-

off leaving
us as Lot'

s little
chance for

turn
ing back.

That first

movement
(Stamitz)

so virtuo
so that I

kept clutch
 ing my own

fingers to
make certain

they were
still hold

ing fast-
to-place.

Do women

change dress
es so often

to-keep-up
with their

chang
ing time

s-of-per
son.

It's only

when girls

reach puberty
that their

nakedness
becomes as

self-reveal
ing as Eve'

s apple–
time.

Haydn'

s "Roxelaine"
symphony (63)

kept him
on his thea

ter's edge
rhyming

quicker than
any such word

s could im
ply.

He couldn'

t see through
the leaves

that window
ed his self-

withhold
ing time's

escaping
moment

s.

Halberstadt 1942

the church

bells bright
ly ringing

the Jews lin
ing up out

side with
those sharp

dead-eyed
dogs A hymn in

tuned to "The
Führer" and

perhaps even
as Christ lined-

up with their
being marched–

off to that
dreaded no–re

turn station.

Evil'

s its own

source grow
s out of

itself The
more it is

the more it
becomes as

weeds desola
ting those

fields allur
ingly beauti

fied.

Agreed

to disagree

whatever
said She took

the opposite
end as an o

pen place dis
tancing

from its e
ver-more va

cating cen
ter.

Completed

When the

poem's com
pleted just

those right
ly-chosen

words stand
ing on their

own im
movably stat

ued.

Either or

How much can

be destroyed
(as those

German cit
ies at the

end of the
war) in

stilled with
a renewing

strength Or
as a desert

steadily in
habiting

those fertile
fields of

ours.

Contrasts (2)

a) Königsberg

He got back

(illegal
ly) via an

untried route
to the city

of his birth
that wasn't

anymore left
to remind

him that it
once-had

been.

b) That little

town in Sile
sia his mother

detailed all
that had been

lost to their
return still

samed house
village

church.

Chernobyl

Didn't you

see all those
butterflie

s bright and
coloring

the forests
still as

dense as if
death could

have silenc
ed those

three-tail
ed swallows

Everything
as it was

almost invis
ibly chang

ed.

Stone-deaf?

but some

stones do
hear vibrat

ing our feel
inged–touch

ed reminder
of what has

happen
ed there'

s no silen
cing them.

These poem

s are like

the world
hadn't happen

ed until now
suddenly

as wind–
storms

became.

Baudelaire

left me level
led with those

sound–image
s of fallen

truths pedest
alled as myth

s of a last
ingly forsak

en world–
sense.

Answering Baudelaire

There may be

beauty in the
simple–every

day But ugli
ness belong

s as little
there as the

most attract
ive of weed

s invading
the composure

of a careful
ly manicured

flower–bed.

The summer

night slow

ed to where
only stars

realizing
the silent

depths of
time's pass

ing.

Slow movement

s rightly sens

ing the soul
of the moon'

s reflect
ive beauty.

This autumn

al fruit

hanging
just as hard

as its unrip
ened touch–

formed.

Haydn's Prestos

The stop-
start's inter

play of un
evened voice-

lengthed a
Haydnes

que rolli
cking finale.

Soft leaf

ed flow

ed an idle
summer day

dreamily
shadow

ing.

First even

ing of feel

ing the light
and shift

ing shadow
s of quite

resembling
eye-length

s.

The stream'

s running

stones light-
transform

ing space-
sounds.

Good marriage

s face the

growing fear
of a one-sid

ed departure
Deathed to

a loss of
one's own i

dentity-
finds.

Good reading

s overcome

us as wave
s of shore

less drift
ings into a

sea of tide–e
voking remem

brance
s.

When he

heard that

his father
had died

That naked
wall at his

end–of–view
became color

lessly alive
to death it

self.

Rashamon

What happen

ed (that robb
er's hold–

up) all–at–
once more per

soned than i
magined simul

taneously
all–truthed.

New friend

s with bound

aries not –
yet–fully

drawn to what
could be said

(and what
not) mind-

touching
each other'

s no-wheres-
but-now.

He couldn'

t exactly ex

press (how
ever precise)

what would al
ways remain

untouchab
ly blurred

from undue re
membrance.

The past

only become

s that when
even dream

can't re
solve its dis

tancing us.

When the

dialogue

stopped as
rivers that

outran them
selves in

to that dried-
down summer-

spell.

Seeing's

She lived

with picture
s of their

together
ness–past as

if the image
of what once-

was could re
appear a

live-seeing.

Relativism

The wisdom

of the Ponti
us Pilate's

signify
ing all-the-

known-ways-
of-man ("what

is truth")
But that only

one encompass
ing a kingdom

far beyond
the reach e

ven of man'
s unquieted

yet ever-quest
ioning mind-

sense.

On-the-run

He was always

on-the-run
as if life

was some
thing to be

caught up–
to until those

stairs turned–
the-tables

of his fall
ing to the

bottom-down
of a lesser

self.

This row of

windows clear–
facing all

those untold
truths that

time has re
frained

from ask
ing why.

At first

we couldn'

t find-her-
out that on–

her–own kind–
of–woman

But what
"her own"

seemed contin
uously chang

ing direct
ions as if

she couldn'
t find her

self out for
more than a

momentary
glimpse.

He was most

ly there for

her not be
ing there

for him A
marriage

like a car
oussel for

all those ar
tificial

lights turn
ing only

their self-
same direct

ion on op
posite

horses each
circling

round an in
visible

center.

The beach

(however dis

tantly it
seemed just

now) still
walking our

tideless
ly stepped im

pression
s disappear

ing at high-
tide (wash

ed over) but
somehow

increasing
ly there.

Some storie

s (not even

the best of
them) like

Willa Cather'
s "Paul"

refuse to be
erased from

their search
ing our inner-

most needs
mostly in

vain.

In memory Charles Seliger

Is each day

like a blank
canvas fill

ed-in with
color

ing design
s just right

for to
morrow's

continuous
ly refin

ing.

That closed-

in air–tight
therapy

still runn
ing back

wards from
time to why

you may never
again inhale

the fresh
ness of spring–

like blossom
ings.

Not yet stone-engraved

She looked

as if she'
d just come

out of the
grave bend

ing over that
death-invok

ing face of
her trying to

find the right
foot forward

but not yet
stone–engrav

ed.

Precious

jewels with

out the beau
ty of a woman

to design
their glow

ing touch
ed as precise

ly as words
strung to the

meaning of
their self-i

dentifying
singular–

sense.

Age

should mean

a slowing
down to time'

s inherent
pulse –

(or is that
only decept

ively true)
that time chang

es with us its
length-for-be

ing.

If a sheep

never forget

s its master'
s voice Why

have we
(helpless

against the
evil within

and the re
lentless

claims of
death) re

mained so deaf
to the voice

of our once-
called master.

If man's

the measure

of all thing
s Why haven'

t we sourced
the cosmos to

its unlimit
ed heights

and plunged
the depths

of the seas
to our all–

consuming
nets And where

is the man
who has har

nassed love to
his own myster

ious claims and
stood up to

death from the
face of his

lonely barren
tomb.

The richness

of Victoria'

s harmonie
s opens

depths of
boundless

spiritual
coloring

s.

Flutter

ing like chic

ken's feeding
teen-age

girl's gigg
ling respon

ses.

Spitzweg'

s cactus lov

er dialog
uing each o

ther's bend
ing uniform

ity with
out even the

needling of
bristling

response
s.

The stealthy

cat's claw

ing-eyed
tree-search

ing the taste
for that in

nocent bird–
flying blood.

Temptation

What's not

allowed (out
of bounds)

that forbidd
en fruit en

larging its
scope over

her juicy in
stincts for

an all-envel
loping taste.

Dementia

Slowly dis

solving from
her emotion

ally-command
ing thought

s melting
down from

that secur
ing hold of

words at the
end but a

voiceless
shadow

ing self.

The surgeon'

s feeling

too much o
ver that fin

er-feel of
his delicate

ly prepar
ing knife

can blood e
ven the cho

sen path
s to his

self-secur
ing hold.

It's only

then on an
open summer

night that
one could bare

ly hear the
stars distan

cing those
self-seeking

thought
s of his.

Same place

same time
even a fam

ilarity of
sense-touch

ing aloud
until those

words could
become dis

tinctly heard.

Poems from Sirmione (7.10.2011)

This soft

morning breeze
and the si

lent ways of
these night-ab

sorbing wave
s thorough

ly calming
that inner

voice of his
time-receiv

ing-self.

Do we

at time
s write with

certain per
sons in mind

as if it
was their con

ceiving just
those perfect

ly chosen im
pression

ed words.

As smoke

rarely phas
ing the trans

parent morn
ing light

a linger
ing impress

ion of an
early roman

tic trio'
s inner-voic

ed reced
ings.

As there'

s a special
flavor to

certain as
pects of French

culture a
taste a scent

a sensual
ity of mind-

impression
s.

If one

can't com

pletely va
cation one

self out
from those

lasting or
still-linger

ing impress
ions envelop

ing in wave
s of a no–

wheres–else.

Children'

s inquisi

tive hands
not quite cer

tain of their
own why or

wherefore
of a touch

ing object'
s seldom mut

ed response.

This heat

today ex

ceeding the
sensibili

ties of
thought or

even touch
ed–causali

ties.

When a wo

man loses her
looks and her

eyes forsake
their self–

appealing so–
defining

Rachel–glance
Does she try

to retrieve
another source

of what may
be ageless

ly self–accom
odating.

Marquis von O *(Kleist)*

Even true

stories in
Kleist's off-

centered
malleable

imaginat
ion often ex

ceed the
bounds of plau

sible human ex
pectation

s.

Are those

unsettling
winds and

their time-dri
ven waves

messaging
us beyond

these moun
tain's irre

vocable stance.

The gull

as a peace
able symbol

after the
storm calm–

climbing
to the height

of its va
cantly ex

posing white
ness.

Is the un

touchable

beauty of
these time

less Graecaen
statues call

ing us back
to a wondrous

time and place
they'd al

ways been sear
ching out for

their own.

Each (for Warren)

> "real poem"
>
> rewrites the
> language
>
> of its own in
> effable
>
> source.

Can birds

> reaching out
>
> such a si
> lent night
>
> that even
> their shadow
>
> s escaping
> those forbidd
>
> en realms of
> touch.

A distant

> steamboat
>
> soundless
> ly retriev
>
> ing its ap
> parent wind–
>
> kept course.

The summer'

s mid–after

noon fullness
that we wonder

why age has
ripened us

so timeless
ly reveal

ing.

Is there

an Austrian

form of mus
ic not so

strong so ab
stract as

the German
but elastic–

lyrically
self–confin

ing a dia
logued idiom

all–its–own.

Early morn

ing-swim cool

ed with the
dark-dream

ed waves of
night's star

less awaken
ings.

Snap-

shot momentar

ily transcen
ding even

that paper
ed smile of

theirs.

The white

ness of swan'
s timeless

ly phrasing
their own ac

cords of tran
scending

light.

Lizard

slither

ing past its
stone–cold

vibration
s.

Peachy'

s your juicy
full–tast

ing gladness–
smile.

It's the

feel of one'

s own feel
ing a voice

vibrating
its depth

ed–through
calling

s.

Mao Tse-Tung

thrashing

the color
s out of liv

ing flower
s as if mind

s could be
left bleeding

from a want
of natural

beauty.

The sparrow' *(for Warren)*

s not a gram

marian But he
does punctu

ate his hop–
flight to

those inbet
ween commas

reassert
ing relative

clauses un
til landing

the full–stop
period's more

much–of–the
same.

The soft-

feel of wave
s called to

an impend
ing shore

left him
with those

speechless
sounds of

time's re
peating cause.

This pebble

d shore's a

residue of
its less–spok

en silence
s.

Kleist'

s short stor

ies so power
fully unin

habited with
unreal per

sons and what-
couldn't-have-

happened self-
realizing.

A long

the beach

Piers suspend
ing the sea–

length of
their unrecor

ded timeless
echoing

s.

The sky'

s blue-clear

ings a clos
ed density

of clouds as
a drama cur

tained to
its finali

zed no–more–
than.

Dual identities

The work-

self and
that vacat

ioned-one'
s self-dual

identit
ies of a

less-unison
ed becoming.

Railing'

s grasping

more of his
mind than

his hands im
prisoned

in those
hold-on

thought
s-of-his.

These hill

s folding in

to a lyrical
expanse

of long-for
gotten

though time
less longing

s.

Thought-

poems should

be dressed
in those or

namental de
signs of

casual self-
deception

s.

For Tommy

Good servant

s however
tempered

must master
the art of

self-denial.

He

couldn't

catch up
to himself

being shadow
ed always

a step be
hind.

"All-the-time-in-the-world"

He had "all–

the–time–in–
the–world" but

not enough
for his litt

le room that
one could

claim had be
come a–world–

unto–itself.

The way

he chose

left no way
of return

Life paths
its own fu

ture leave
s some of us

stranded on a
one-way pre-

signed course.

"Caught-his-eye"

She "caught-

his-eye" like
a fish lined

to its baited-
holding

for only the
bringings

in.

A tiny girl

with a broad-

blue-hat sat
delicate

ly on the
beach feed

ing a family
of ducks as

if her world
centered

to her very-
touch just–

then.

She too small

her father
too tall

that she
could hard

ly look-up
to his tower

ing over
her very-source

d being.

Descenzano'

s stone-bred

image time
lessly arisen

across the
lake's se

cretly rhy
med aware

nesses.

Origins

Could it

have been
the continu

ity of those
muted though

insistent
waves that

voiced him
with self-re

sounding rhy
thms.

These

off-set flow

ers rail-
way stripp

ed breath
lessly

blooming
their wind-

resisting
colors.

Soft bree

zes the quiet

reach of
clouds and

the warmth
of an Ital

ianate sum
mer day un

isoned him
to a tired

ness depthed
as deeply

within that
unrelingu

ishing sun.

A lone

bird circl

ing a height
well beyond

its own
sense of time'

s distanc
ing cause.

Imitations

She became

so used to i
mitating

what she'd
seen that one

could well–as
sume she'd

become dress
ed in second–

hand appear
ances.

It's often

    the other-side-

    of words (their
    unblemish

    ed appear
    ances) that

    must be found
    out A hide–

    and–seek
    game of or

    iginally
    there.

Each mea

    sured step

    he took con
    cealing the e

    choes of his
    less–reveal

    ing thought
    s.

The lake

slept those

night–wind
s through

Not even
the innumer

able stars
could awaken

its unseen
presence.

This tree

leafed in

numerable
thoughts

satiated
from time'

s repeated
(though

still un
heard)

calling
s.

If

the dove'

s a symbol
of peace

able forth
coming time

s Why does
it fly so

far above
these trans

cending re
solves of

mine.

Dual-identity

This almost

wintered
coarse-bark

ed tree's
as the grave

features of
aging-resol

ute men still
standing up

to their green-
apparent pre

sense.

The veins

> of his
>
> through–de
> ciding hand
>
> s as leave
> s windless
>
> ly time–ex
> posing.

That low-

> pressured
> look about
>
> his having
> been taken
>
> down to such
> a heavily–
>
> impending
> sadness.

These wa

> ters stone–
>
> pebbled their
> glimmering
>
> coolness
> through.

Bellini'

s Madonna

s so pure
ly classical

ly conceiv
ed a contempla

tive silence o
vercoming

all that o
therwise

ness of time
and place.

When the weep

ing willow let

the full-length
of her hair

down All those
sadnesses re

leased to the
wind's time

less remembran
ces.

When

words become

more shell
and the sound

s of the sea
singing

through
those dead–

silence
s down–deep.

A city at

dawn its hou

ses so still
that I could

barely hear
their listen

ing aloud
to that full–

moon fad
ing slowly

from light.

These cut-

off branch

es wounded
from growth as

soldiers
after the war

limbed only to
painful re

membran
ces.

Sense-for-view

That little

girl bare
ly find

ing her feet
still com

ing on by
coloring

her dress to
my own sense-

for-view.

Some place

> s don't
>
> change left–
> behind as that
>
> little Schles
> ian town with
>
> the rooms
> (all those
>
> years)
> cultivat
>
> ing a tradit
> ion of same
>
> ness.

For Rosemarie

> The older
>
> we become
> the more of
>
> us binds so
> intricate
>
> ly together
> Time rare
>
> ly relinguish
> es what it
>
> has called
> to a oneness
>
> of now self–
> encompassing
>
> that always–
> then.

Boats at

anchor call

ing the tide
s into their

night-time
recurring

depthed-si
lences.

Outframed

The same

scene as a
picture per

manently
framed the

lake boats
trees but

these cloud
s moving the

wave's lessen
ing-from-flow.

Each little

poem if un

said would
leave some

thing miss
ing an o

pened space
however

tiny would
hurt at some

unknown
source.

Her dark

glasses al

ways present
a part of

her person
ed–self as

if to pro
tect from

what other
s might ex

pose within
darkly con

cealing.

So much

had been gi

ven the fear
of loss had

become a part
of his daily

bread a counter-
rhythm blood

ed deeply with
in defying

the why and
wherefore of

his very-be
ing.

Each day

lived to the

fullest
as if time

was running
out on him

drying down
as those

summer-tim
ed southern

streams.

A chance-

meeting they

called it
(as some

far-fetched
random a

side)
as if "chance"

hadn't taken
on a calling

all-its-own.

He sat

so long at

the water'
s edge feel

ing those
self-reclaim

ing waves
softly through

until the lake'
s rhythm had

become a gen
tle part of

his own.

He heard

those step

s coming e
ver–closer

shadow
ing the very–

depth of his
being im

mersed in what
wasn't any

more.

Market

day all–aflash

of color'
s sound

ing out inex
plicit shadow

ing form
s.

Evil'

s a repetit

ion of its
own being

always on
coming.

That slow-

tide steam

boat slow
ing down to

the wave
s of his own

linger
ing thought–

flows.

Left behind

Where he left

those cloud–
like dream

s behind
their length

of seeing be
yond his own

self–reali
zings.

Schnitzler'

s closely–

felt stories
at the pulse

of knowing
why those

times (and e
ven he him

self) a
drift with

out an anchor
ing–hold.

We witness

ed only those
muted feather

s bloodless
ly left be

hind the re
mains of what

we dared not
imagine.

When

Schnitzler

lost all
his marriage

in ruins his
favorite

daughter
dead at her

own hands
his hearing

fading to
the coming

tragedy of
his times so

deeply self–
personed.

Only love

can redeem

this faith
less world–of–

our–own mak
ing mapped

out to those
finer denial

s of a self–
finding alone

liness.

Judged wrong

too much of
his own and

too little of
the other

clouding out
that land

scaping of
mostly un

known shore
s.

The ambigu

ity of stair

s leading up
or down not

knowing the
where of his

own direction
less path.

Descenzano

that myster

ious mediev
al city of

narrow
ly abandon

ed street
s leading e

ver-deeper
into the

realms of
their unre

corded past.

The boat

waved to

why time'
s passing it

self slowly
by Here only

shadowed re
membrance

s.

Always now

If time

could always
be only–

now only–
here an is

land of our
selves salvag

ed from the
teeming sea

and the tide
less current

s of these shift
ing times Here

in the mid–sum
mer of our ag

ing years
stopped only–

now only–then.

Early morn

ing these

water–bird
s wingèd

with light–
surfacing

the farthest
reaches of

sound.

This pier

foot-sens

ing my read
ied thought

s minnow
ing the light

of their lost–
found echo

ing appeal
s.

That stealthy

cat over there
blackened

in blood
ied thought

s clawed–down
to its basic

flesh–instin
cts.

That cat

(again) those

waking-glar
ing eyes of

his being
feathered to

the taste of
dead-bird'

s bloodied
cries.

Seagull

s innocent

ly cloud-per
suading

the light-
waves of this

morning's
gracious a

wakenings.

Klee'

s malicious

cat resurfa
cing my mind'

s eager aware
nesses.

Wolfgang

They knew it

would happen
"You could see

it coming on"
they said

(only after
it did)

not it but
him (seeming

ly "normal")
until he dis

appeared that
night into

those all-im
mersing wood

s.

For Rosemarie

My love for

you as those
softly car

essing wave
s called gen

tly into the
silent touch

of their mu
ted realm

s-of-shore.

Age was diff

erent see

ing it or be
ing it seem

ed so distant
then some

thing that
happens to o

thers hard–of–
hearing see

ing walking–
strides hamper

ed by a bro
ken step

Now it live
s inside me

as a caged
feeling of

nowheres
out.

Beauty

so uneased

my Uncle Ir
ving off–balan

cing him as
a height too

remote to be
taken down to

the every
day of his

work-sheet pa
pered-over

life.

A rooster

at the top

of the church
roof wind-re

minding the
few of Peter'

s steadfast
denials.

Right-there

As the cam

era focuses
so does the

mind until
it's right-

there depth
ed-in no

wheres else.

The poetic

voice was

once-heard
here Catullus

between love
and hate-wave

s overcom
ing those dis

tances of
height and

time plying
the stone bea

ches' ever-re
minding

lonely
poetic call.

At Catullus' Grotto

This vast

ly surround
ing sea circl

ing one in
to the

schrubb
ed-down grass

of overlast
ing timed-

accords.

Close to

the scent of

wild animal
s He earthed-

out the prim
itive calling

s of residual
blood-instinct

s.

He knew

he was be

ing watched
from a strange

ly distant
source that

pulled magnet
ically tight

as a fish
lined to its

helpless
cause.

Poem'

s only when

words recreate
the form of

what's be
ing seen.

Surfers

skimming

the waves
wind–delight

ed balance
ing between

light and
sound.

Chance

meeting

s as run–
down thought

s hard to
place allus

ively tran
sitional.

This morn

ing's moon

as the fa
ding thought

s of dream'
s misplaced

moments
scarcely de

fining.

Brought-down

My grand

father the
King Lear

command
ing over his

need-to-be-o
bedient

rightly fear
ed brought-

down child
ren.

Incomplete *(Mozartean)*

What's left

incomplete
an empti

ness at the
wordless

heart of va
cantly un

realized
meaning.

As a dog

who couldn'

t find his
own tail

searching
the scent of

life that paw
ed him in

to indeli
cate expos

ures.

Light-vows

Thousand
s of birds

practis
ing for flight

reclaiming
the heavens

anew for their
cold–emanci

pating light-
vows.

Inch-worm

eating up

the leave
s of his fine

ly-thread
ed downness

es.

Quick ans

wers that brush-

aside manner
for less endear

ing question
s as a woman

veiled in post-
nightly ex

pressive
ness.

She seemed

as those grown

swans who hadn'
t changed co

lors into
their complete

whiteful
ness.

Listen

ing to two

voices the
sea and his

own until
they slowly

merged voice
lessly.

The swan

sailing its
white-attun

ed elegance
unaware of

the quiet
ing flow of

such unseen
admiring

beauty.

That pleas

ure steamer

all white
and festive

ly sailing
the length

of this lake'
s summering

flag-flutter
ing gladness

es.

Waiting *(for Ingo and Solvey)*

when it may

be a question
of life or

death when
waiting be

comes an in
visible voice

less person
almost omni

sciently
reigning o

ver space and
timeless

ly unheard.

The sparr

ow hop-measur

ing short-lined
space to the

feel-touch
of tiled

floor-sens
ing nearness

es.

Hands-on-hip

self-reass

uring statu
esquely posed

as if draw
ing the tide

s into
knowing who

was command
ing right-here

right-now.

Closed-off

Even now at

the height
of summer

those all–im
mersing shad

ows closing
in on us –

There's no
way out as the

impending
mountains

have closed–
off all possi

ble means of
escape.

Ghettoed

its walls pro

tectively
high Enemied

on all sides
a world with

in a world
waiting for

a God who
chooses his

own time.

He was

quick with pro

mises but slow
to remember

Some thought
it was his

intense way
of doing

things But
others felt

he was too
tacted to his

own sail
s.

Is that

really me

That old man
half-hobbl

ing up the
stairs hold

ing tight
to the rail

ing for supp
ort It's not

the way I
feel but it

feels me out
so!

Are these

steady–contin

uous rains
washing our

times away
as if clean

sing them
of all those

threaten
ing memorie

s sea–deep.

These wave

> s the always–
>
> now timeless
> ly rhymed to
>
> their in-flow
> ing rhythm
>
> ic appearan
> ces.

These wave

> s dream-like
>
> memories
> reaching
>
> through
> those shore
>
> s of eternal
> forgetful
>
> ness.

A boat

> drift
>
> ing those
> sound
>
> less distan
> ces as morn
>
> ing moon'
> s time-fa
>
> ding.

"What does it mean"

as if mean

ing was only
one-eyed

stripped of
its persis

tently recall
ing image and

the grace
fullness of its

musically–
rhythmic ac

cords.

Unseen

He looked

as if he did
n't know where

his eyes on
the move fo

cusing more
on what he

didn't see.

Why so often

poemed be

cause it has
n't all been

said These ten
sions at the

heart of word–
releasing.

Some need

their high–

horse to be
saddled rhetor

ically over–
weighted Mine

prefers to be
watered in

those shaded
silences of

intimate
ly spell–

bound.

Portraiture *(3)*

a) Is it the

painter'

s concept
of what is

to be seen
sensed–reali

zed as if
all his portr

aits become
more or less

self-portrait
s Or is his

more a dia
logue of

"I and thou"
inbecoming

mysterious   ´
ly self-reali

zing.

b) "The mind's eye"

If we see

more with
the mind

than the
eye as if

we're more
than for appear

ance sake
(then) what

appears may
not be that

person at all
or more-of-him

than he could
possibly real

ize.

c) *"No man's an island"*

Do we change

what we see
because we'

re the one
seeing it

(if so)
I'm only a

part of my
mirroring

self while o
thers may mir

ror more of
themselve

s than of my
being-me.

If Stephen

Foster "found

out" the Sw
anee river

(never hav
ing been

there him
self) Then

that river
isn't water

ed at all but
more an un

realizing
dream-sense.

A lone table

once people

d but no long
er than its

depth of uni
fying self—

contain
ment.

"Just pull yourself together"

they said as

if some part
s of him had

loosened–out
and left most

of the other
s incoherent

ly self–in
volving.

The short–

breathed

sparrow (as
some persons

I've known)
never try to

exceed their
pre–ordain

ed range–of–
possibili

ties.

A jewel

must be re

fined to the
intricate

source of
its light–ap

parent bright
ness.

That scottie's

s watchful

ears uplift
ing his in

herent sense
of awareness

to the pitch
ed height

s of an a
wakened–

readiness.

The ugli

ness of age

misformed
appearan

ces can re
veal an inner

off-natural
beauty But

uglifying'
s destruct

ive of God'
s own beauti

fying creat
ive power

s.

White gull

s time-sus

pending wing
èd at light'

s dawn.

Landscaped

It's only

when the land
begins to

speak land
scaping

the flow of
our envelop

ing hills and
the depth of

our sound
less waters

that we become
attuned to

that other in
lasting voiced-

self.

Sirmione

castled us

into those
remotely

shadow
ing memor

ies of its e
vasively-

escaping med
ieval past.

When the

morning a

wakens one
could almost

sense the
breath of

its always–
renewing

light.

For Neil

At the end

of the road
It's when our

tentative
steps reced

ing into
those unheard

realms of con
templative

leisure
we begin to

realize
life–itself'

s continu
ously a no–

turning–
back.

Secrets

We all harbor

our own self–
revealing se

crets But those
deepest and

darkest remain
mostly hidden

from our own
activating

self.

Accountability *(S. L.)*

He saw it

his way and
I mine

But it re
mained as it

always appear
ed a samed–

otherwise
ness inescap

ably poised.

Squirrel

ling the hide-

and–seek of
catch–me–up

down–swing
ing up–end

ings of no–
wheres–from

here.

Remaining

true to one'

s theorie
s the death–

bed of stag
nant water

s.

Hail

stones dan

cing a quick
ening repeti

tive pace
that left him

cooling–for–
breath.

With friend

s dying and

those griev
ed from more

than life
could reclaim

we somehow
feel island

ed–assured
but fearful

for waiting.

After the

storm one

senses light
again as a

jewel spark
ling through

the touch of
its self–de

ciphering
facet

s.

Starred

How many

held on to
their only i

dentity
here (as Lot'

s wife) star
red to those

six-pronged
death's un

failing re
solve.

For Ingo

4 days in a

timeless
void hang

ing beween
life and death

powerless to
fight back as

if another
hadn't long–

before decid
ed the out

come of that
unequall

ed dual.

If "he

wasn't him

self" than
whose self

had he be
come And if

he came back
to his "real

self" dis
covering a

gain as if
nothing had

really chang
ed?

Discoverings (for George)

If we're

(as Fleming
and Columbus)

mostly dis
covering

what we weren'
t looking for

Maybe it
would be best

if we start
ed out look

ing for what
we wouldn'

t have been
looking for

in-the-first-
place.

At times

one can al

most feel the
seeing-strength

of a dark
ness inhabit

ing more of
this world

(and of one
self) unspok

en yet threat
ening.

Hommage à Kafka

This hospital

more a labyrin
th for get

ing lost from
the patient

s don't know
what the nurse

s doesn't either
what the doc

tors perhap
s haven't

yet found a
way for diag

nosing the
wrong patient.

Prayers *(3)*

a) It's not

what one see

s but how
one sees it

A tree re
mains simply

a tree for
shadows in

wind or light–
releasing

leaves Lord
help us to

see not what
but how You

have taught
us.

b) A salmon

on–the–line

shouldn't
be held too–

tight or he'
ll break free

Nor should we
give him too–

much line or
he'll spit

the hook out
Lord I thank

you for hav
ing caught me

in just that
right–kind–

of–way.

c) I don't

know what

all these
windows are

seeing They'
re looking

through glass
to bring that

light in
Lord if it'

s really
light that

they've been
seeing then

make me to
a window

of your un
seen being.

Space

is when

birds open
ing their

wings to
those light–

felt distan
cings.

The beauty

of those

leafless
bared–down

wintered
trees as

Adam and Eve
so nakedly

hiding from
their own

self–reveal
ing thirst

for a higher
cause.

Tolerance

Today's toler

ance but an
emptied–face

allegiance
to one's own

lack–of–con
viction.

The tribute Money *(Titian 1515, Dresden)*

Jesus and the

Pharisees so
closely knot–

together hand
s eyes communi

cating in
their own per

sonal unspok
en language

that only
that–coin

in the midd
le shining

with the lus
ter of an im

perial glance–
dividing them

darkly apart.

To make sense

of a world

circling out
side its pre–

given bound
aries as that

plague–ship
1349 sailing

to port with
only rats gnaw

ing at the
helm.

Cezanne'

s still life

s that won'
t stay still

tensioned
at the source

of a center
less unity.

Brueghel'

s children'

s games mi
micing the pre-

dawn to adult'
s world-aware

nesses.

At these

sit–down–time

s of aging
It's hard

(believe me)
to stand for

most anything
except those

breathers
simulating

time–expand
ing interval

s sometime
s referred

to as "poem".

Small and

chaste rose

s in the
cool light

of calmed-in
ward contem

plation
s.

Schnitzler'

s closely-

touched feel
for the inner

thoughts
and mostly

desires of
others too

close to his
own (self-

defending)
weakness

es.

"Pomp and Circumstance"

was more his

way (with
pawned cloth

and gown) of
a continu

ously self-
supporting

reverence.

Apples

repeating

that self-
same cycle

of ripen
ing these

times in
to the juicy

(but poison
ed taste)

of man's on
coming fall.

"Let's remain

in continu

ous dialogue"
meant that

crafty spid
er to the

tiny fly
caught in

his fragile
ly taste

ful net.

Those

consumed

by loneli
ness and loss

should real
ize how the

smallest of
flowers long

s for even
the slight

est touch-of
light.

For Rosemarie

A woman'

s beauty
must be kiss

ed blossom
ing those pro

mising flower
s from one'

s own encour
aging lips.

The bells

of that dis

tant church
ringing out

the morning'
s bright

ness but few
came to real

ize why.

Mirandolina *(4)* *(Goldoni)*

a) defending

her own sense-
of-freedom

and her fa
ther's will

playing with
men's vanit

ies until
they became

slaves to
their own in

ordinate de
sires.

b) Mirandolina'

s perfect

ly self-ful
filling marr

iage with
her servant

always ready
to comply with

her daily de
mands and de

sires.

c) If great

art remain

s timeless
Why need Mir

andolina be
sexed–up

to a decay
dent untell

ing burles
que.

d) The main

character

her fa
ther never

came on stage
And yet he

determined
Mirandol

ina's very–
being as my

own mother
once said

her long–dead
father was

still–watch
ing over her

every–decis
ion.

When a

kiss retain

s the frag
rance of that

indwelling
rose.

Looking

at picture

s of the
dead paper–

smiling
though still

inhabiting
a timeless

ly life–like
appearance.

Tchaikovsky'

s first quar

tet (not the
highly emotion

ally–charged
colored–work

s I'd become
so used to)

But lyrical
ly self–sus

taining its
shifting

mood–invok
ing tonalit

ies.

An unreal world

When the fog

s came in
transform

ing even one'
s own breath

into the
realms of an

unreal world
only the

warmth of
touch could

realize the
oneness of

our own per
sonal-self.

The heroic

ideal may

have died
(here in Eur

ope) a
bloody death

on the battle
field But its

favored com
poser still

spirits not
only those

muscle-mind
ed youths

But middle-
aged lean-

chair aesthet
es as well.

Flower

s withered

to the death-
encumber

ed dryness
of their

grave-ston
ed appear

ance.

Whose child which way

When her

only child
learned to

love Christ
more than her

self She com
plained "you'

ve taken my
child away

from me"
Whose child?

which way?

Outlived

He outlived

Auschwitz
though Ausch

witz outliv
ed him as

an artifi
cial sunflow

er dried–down
bloomed–out.

"Cultural

Christians" as

"cultural Jews"
are like prett

ied inborn
flowering

s dead–at–
the-roots.

Animal prayers (3)

a) Fish's prayer

Lord I can
only speak to

You by mirr
oring those

unspoken si
lent-depth

s.

b) Frog's prayer

I jump Lord

I wouldn't
want to fly

like the bird
s as if hea

venly bound
nor creep like

those lowly
creature

s No Lord
I jump these

inbecoming
prayers

to You.

c) Mouse prayer

4 main street

s 3 lesser
side-ones

12 holes all
in 6-and-a-

half-minute
s I thank You

Lord that I
can create

quicker
than any

thoughts
I might

squeak
these hidden

prayers to
You deeply

within my pro
tective hide-

outs.

"We are all guilty" (4) *(Goethe 1769)*

a) Two unseen

actors stand

ing high-a
bove those

on-stage The
10 command

ments and the
power-of-for

giveness creat
ing a heaven

ly answer to
man's guilt–

contriving
self.

b) The end

may have fit

the action
but not the

actors – Sophie
confined to

a lifeless
ly all-con

suming life
with the

wrong hus
band.

c) Sophie'

s father

with an in
fallible in

stinct for
making the

wrong decis
ions.

d) Alceste

for all his

romantic
charm and ca

vallier-be
havior al

ways on the
outside of

what he most-
desired.

"Don't tell

me what I

don't want to
hear" –

Too much of
the bare and

barren truth
leaves behind

but a desolate
landscap

ing loveless
ly inhabit

ed.

These sum

mer winds re

main unseen
leaf-remind

ing of
their touch

ing color-
changes.

The Doubt *(Caravaggio)*

ing Thomas
could only be

lieve what
he felt-touch

ed to his fin
ger's insist

ing faith-deny
ing urge.

Schnitzler

couldn't

trust women
because he

couldn't
trust himself

while Goethe
pedestall

ed them so
high oft far–

beyond his own
far-reaching

cause.

Repeat per

formances

like the neo–
classical

bloodless
ly self-en

during.

Abandoned

when these

mountain
streams run-

down their
stone-bared

dryness
Vacantly a

bandoning
the depth of

their over-com
ing cause.

"Making con

versation"

The fear of
not saying

anything
That word

less void
speaking

tensely a
loud Hurts.

Pfungstadt I

Those aband

oned Jewish
houses not

torn-down
not even re

inhabited
but left as

they were
ghost-like-

alive to their
immutable

past.

Pfungstadt II

That night-

of-crystal
s the befrien

ded Jewish
shop-keeper

s plundered
out of all

self-respect
left.

The mist

slowly re

treating in
to those

cloud-drift
ing heaven'

s nowhere
s-from-now.

Isaiah 41

I couldn'

t quite place-
him puzzled

with too
many emptied

spaces as if
there could

be no-other-
place left

than his.

"Soul-mate"

s they call

ed it as if
pre-designed

to an unknown
(and yet)

familiar
sense-

calling.

Tersteegen' (for Thomas)

s mystical

quietude
s so private

ly remote
to a finer

intimate
sense-from-

being.

Always becoming

When time

s flow in
to a cloud-

increasing
always becom

ing.

He was like

a king on an

emptied
throne young

alert–look
ing with a

healthy smile
that obscur

ed the vacant
ness of his

heart–beat
being.

Boredom'

s closer to

a kingdom
of the dead

Nothing breath
es there as

times have
been emptied–

out increas
ingly roomed

in uninhab
ited chair

s and those
private

ly-felt sha
dowings al

ways self-e
choing.

The daily

passing of

our burial
grounds leave

s me a bit
more stone-in

scribed than
these paper

ing accord
s could just

ly reclaim.

As you like it *(Shakespeare) (3)*

a) "I'm not what I am"

If we change

how we appear
and live that

role long e
nough (per

haps) we'd
become more

of what we
aren't.

b) Ship-wrecked

dead or a

live they
could start a

new as those
missing af

ter the war
But how few

could redis
cover what

they weren'
t anymore.

c) Does new

land inhabit

us different
ly as Zion

ism claims or
born-again

Christian
s How far can

we become o
therwise-

from-self.

When and/or

does French
music sound o

therwise or
the darkly

passionate
Russian "soul"

History
(then) is

not the only
why of peo

ple's (at
times disclaim

ing) differ
ences.

For Rosemarie

one of those

few who think
of others

first instinct
ly helping

before their
own keeping

this out-bal
anced most

ly ship-wreck
ed world-of-

ours still sail
ored-afloat.

Freud

asked the

wrong quest
ions It does

n't really
matter *why* we'

re so problem
ed as now

But *how* we
become the

less of our
lonely self.

The turn

ing back to

what we've
left behind

may renew
our lessen

ing claim
s for a fu

ture growth.

If we be

lieve what

we want to
believe then

truth has al
ready turn

ed–the–cor
ner on our

ever straight–
ahead self.

Some town

s awaken in

me strange
The cobbled

streets of
old–town

Bautzen
turned my an

kle in–to
a pained feel

ing for those
imprison

ed there.

Plum

tree ripen

ing into the
juicy color

s of its
moon-touch

persuas
ions.

"He's a poet

you know" that

look on the
dean's quite

regular face
as if an un

known spirit
was float

ing about
the biblical

length of
his holding-

tight to se
cure an ade

quately adept
judgment

seat.

"What's in a name"

as if ours

(however care
fully chosen

to fit some
dead-time re

lative) could
bring-to-life

a pre-expos
ure of our own

time-telling
being.

We knew

we'd never

see each o
ther again

He retreat
ing into

the ever-in
creasing

shadow of
his former

self slow
ly fading a

way from.

Moon-time

the night'

s awaken
ing from the

wood's darken
ing remem

brances.

Giraff'

s self-evol

ing leaf-topp
ed tongue'

s eliciting
tastiness.

The tiger'

s claw-eyed

tasting im
pressions

foot-print
ing its caged–

in instinct
s.

White sail

ing through
the tide

less voice
of Illmensee'

s self-resplend
ent quietud

es.

Dream-spells

Shifting

clouds dark
rains omin

ously immer
sing into

their time-
drifting

dream-spell
s.

Martin'

s very-feat

ures soil-dep
thed the sur

facing claim
s of his ac

cumulat
ing Schwab

ian herit
age.

Light-moments

Birch wood

s graceful
ly ascending

the heaven
ly blue of

their inescap
able light–

moment
s.

Lake rose

s suspending

the water
ing length

of their
withhold

ing colored–
from moment

s.

He desir

ed more but

had to be
satisfied

with less
age-breeding

the limits
to his own

life-source
s.

Wave-messages

The secret

ly intensed
quietude

s of this
through-form

ing lake left
him with only

its slight
ly indecipher

able wave-
message

s.

A fisher

man alone in

the midst of
a self-surr

ounding lake'
s untouched

depth of his
own silenc

ing thought
s.

Little child

ren awared

to a world
still myster

iously un
touched.

This tran

quil early–

morning–sky
blued his a

wakening
thought

s to their
subdued time–

coloring
s.

Martin

timed me

back to a
common world

that hadn't
yet escaped

its purpos
ing claim

s on us.

Raphael

our retarded
son sang him

self into
a world rhy

med and col
ored even be

yond those in
terior realm

s of non-thought
ful express

iveness.

Our friend

s however

diverse in
habiting

this or that
side of our

time-evol
ving self.

Other claims

The claim

s we remem
ber of our

outlasting
childhood

rarely same
ed to those

of their par
entful watch-

ed obser
vances.

Pulled-in by

She usual

ly tried to
better him

with subtle
ly insinuat

ing example
s that he

took-for-his-
own as a fish

hooked to her
steadied

pulling-him-
in-by.

All smiles

that little–

middle-aged–
man happy at

his own happy
thoughts

though retard
ed to his

very-bone.

High

in the tree

s flowing
the leave'

s wind-con
suming pre

sences.

How

Bellini

has flavoured
his own atmos

pheric world
to its inten

sely silenced
heavenly pre

sence.

If painter

s can teach

us to see–a
new and com

posers sound
out the in

terior depth
s of our very–

person we
poets are left

with only
the word'

s redefin
ing craft.

If the invis

ible wind

symbolize
s the Holy

Spirit Its o
ver–earthly

power can des
troy to create –

anew as it
could soften

as with Elijah'
s untold close

ness prayed–
presence.

Are instru

ments voiced

with the tim
bre of their

own special
ly conceiv

ing touch or
are they dia

logued to
our inner

voice-touch
ing self.

Silence

can speak loud

er than word
s of a self-

realizing lov
ed-oneness

or the quiet
udes of an art

encompass
ing those dee

per silence
s of spirit

ually realm
ed.

Baal-be

lief when those
thrusting sex

ual desire
s discolor

ing even deep
er than those

true-blue
encompass

ing realms
s-of-love.

Blond-blue

eyed-naïve

but manly-
through until

the war recre
ated him in

its own i
mage A man

who knew too
much to ever-

again become
so express

ively-near
to what he'

d so lonely
lost.

If they

couldn't

think–big
They could

(at least)
little them

selves to a
detailing

life of per
sonal self–

finding
s.

Secret-historians

He was like

those secret-
historian

s who knew–it–
all through

their anec
dotal eyes

featuring
trivial self–

encompass
ing storie

s.

We knew

they'd been

landscaped
to a dialect

of alb-like
festly-form

ed identi
ties.

Their his

tory (so per

sonally self-
assuming)

more of a sum
mary of this

or that side
of family-in

voking self-
recurren

ces.

After his

wife died

he dialogu
ed himself

into a guilt–
compiling re

collection
of what he

did or didn'
t do most al

ways wrong.

How a friend

ship when ne

glected or
otherwise

harbored
could no

longer flag–
fly differ

ing route
s.

Can one a

wakening

through
dream's star–

lining those
intricate

feelings of
a timeless

ly present-
past.

Brother

and sister

fibered
from those

same-parent
s to an in

ner accord'
s self-suffi

ciency.

Those less

er quality
school–child

ren's song
s awaken in

him to this
very-day poet

ically sens
ed mooned-ton

alities.

The Berlin

wall divid

ing a war–de
feated people

from its his
torical

claims of un
ifying what

had become
but a short–

lengthed
bombed–out

common des
tiny.

Illmensee

through

night–moon
ed waves quiet

ing our reflect
ively sooth

ing response.

Lost hearing

On that
cool–summer–

night He'd
lost hear

ing those
field–invok

ing cricket
s collect

ive recall
ings.

Widening

his sense of

realizing
where those

white gull
s and sails

envelop
ing time–

phases.

Rediscover

ing what could

have been
better-said

those unspok
en word's ir

regular time-
sequencing.

Taking a dis

tance to one

self's more
like those

spaced-pause
s between

touch's af
ter-feeling

s why.

Each day

fully last

ed until no
remembran

ces left ex
cept those

here-now
words.

Afraid

of a world

beyond her
self-certain

ed–reach
hardened as

a tree more
bark than

leaves high–
standing.

She wrote

him "I don'

t know who
I am" as if

any–of–us
could snap–

shot more
than a fac

ial semblan
ce of our mo

mentary
self.

After deaths *(for Martin)* *(4)*

a) When his

wife died
after years

of corres
ponding mean

ings He left
his past

(those un
earthed sha

dowings)
hovering o

ver his pre
vious boundr

ies of ten
tative self–

sufficien
cies.

b) Chung

It wasn't

his wife's
death that

plagued his
over-riding

sense-of-con
science But

his own self–
called failing

at the center
of what he

couldn't
possibly

have done.

c) Karin

She was

more like a
shore resound

ing those
waves of

loss to a
steadied re

newing pulse–
of-presence.

d) Jean

Our too-far–
away to fully

realize her
response to

oneness that
left her lone

ly as a flag
less ship

out–tacted.

It's often

what we did

n't do deter
mining our

life's–span
Those ways

that ended
before they

started
through our

out–boundr
ied self.

Vanhal'

s exquisite

Oboe Quartet
s opus 7

at times more
Mozartean

than Mozart
himself imit

ating his
own self-re

fining puri
fied express

iveness.

For Rosemarie *(50th anniversary)*

For a good

marriage to
succeed one

must daily
court one'

s wife into
that primary

softness of
love's long–

lasting in
tangible

routes.

Horn Trio *(Brahms op. 40)*

A call from

the woods
(Eichendorff)

densed color
ing his taut–

contoured-
mind's sooth

ing express
iveness.

Horn Trio *(Mozart K. 407)*

Mozart'

s purity of
phrasing

the most
natural of

fluent ex
pressive

ness.

Messiaen

encored a sen

sual impress
ionist pur

ity of spaced-
intervall

ed accord
s.

Fritz Kreisler'

s virtuo

so-fingering
a depth

less surfac
ing self-ap

preciation
s.

A summer

that never

fully–became
the sun-warmth

ed fullness
of its call

ing's like a
woman not

yet fully ri
pened to a

need for a
man's fulfill

ing there
ness.

Escape rooms

Lois needed

an escape to a
privacy that

sensitive
teenage girl

s house from
their own

mostly self
closed–in feel

ings.

Women

like Alma Mahler
or George Sand

activate
their own mind–

body needs for
famous men

helpless
ly caught in

their captivat
ing spider–web

bed longing
s.

Bi-lingual

off-ground

s for poets
can never be

come samed–
why words im

ply a vagrant
history of

their own
self–breed

ings.

Bunched

flowers differ

ently color
ed so-tight

ly-kept that
one felt cer

tain Each
would lose its

special scent
under such con

fining condit
ions.

Between

stops one al

most feels
like an in

between per
son neither

here nor there
but always

on the run
as if time

was only
meant to be

caught-up-u
pon.

If I *were*

a woman I

would feel
the earth–like

awakening of
my body as

either prett
ied flower

s ornament
ally dressed

in pattern
s of my own

mind–tending
Or (perhap

s) earth–swell
urges of dark

ening under
ground tempta

tions.

When her (partially in remembrance D. H. Lawrence)

husband
died She felt

(as she said)
physically

unfulfilled
as if they

were bodied
to more (or

less) than the
mind or spirit

could possibly
nourish.

If life'

s the end
then death'

s the creat
or of our own

timeless re
mains God of

the grave
yard's hushed–

reverent si
lence's

stone–inscrib
ing parish.

Soccer *(for Erik)*

his sport

(not played
but seen)

its own aesthet
ic spaced in

rhythmic patt
erns leaving

the eye time–
circling wind–

like.

Games

imitating

more of us
than we real

ize have often
taken the place

of real life
played-out

on a field
clearly mark

ed though bound–
dried by our

own restless
need for

more.

His own dis

colored blood–

streaming
suspicious

of other'
s real–like

motivation
s.

A dulled

late summer

day rained
down to a sky

less appear
ance of no–

wheres–but–
now.

If "life'

s a continu
ous learn

ing process"
It may be

because
the power of

forgetful
ness over

rides us all
as the un

winding of
Penelope'

s suitably
dressed–up

appearan
ces.

The height

of that med

ieval tower
ing over Ster

zing clocked
to a time

less forget
fulness.

As a minis

ter I still

remember
her all-of-

fourteen
fearful/trem

bling need'
s of protect

ing from her
flesh-hungry

father.

Multscher'

s standing

figures
most exquis

itely lyrical
when profil

ed to an in
ner sense of

their own self-
contemplat

ing dignity.

The athletic

-type more

muscle than
minding a

book for crea
tive insight

s bodied a
post-gamed

intimitat
ing swagger.

The sweeping

dress of Mult

scher's annun
ciation lyri

cally reaffirm
ing The Vir

gin's all-en
compassing

"yes".

Summer

in South Italy

at those dead-
streamed si

lences that
lowers even

the blood-flow
of one's own

life-dimin
ishing impul

ses.

Under-voiced

In the heat

of summer we
often seek-

out the sha
dowed realm

s of thought
A right-poem

could cool us
that way with

its shadow
ing intonat

ion's under-
voiced.

This early

morning kept

in secluded
silences se

cretly aware
of its time

lessly always
s–now.

The lake

at dawn se

cretly en
closing the

depth of its
dreamed–

through dark
nesses.

That house

the secret

ly–silent–
one rarely in

habited with
its manicur

ed lawns and
the freshen

ing yellow
of its almost

artificial
ly colored–

awaiting
s.

Some town

s like Scars
dale live
more through

their imper
sonally with

holding fa
cades than

by those
short–term

ed remembr
ances of its

next–stop
uneasing in

habitant
s.

A slight

bird touch

ed-down on
the gnarled

branch of a
dead-leafed

tree in the
midst of a

blooming
summer-green

ed landscape.

He put up

his steel-plat

ed armour to
protect a

gainst the
blood-pain

s of those
hurts still

seeping slow
ly through.

The long

pier foot-step

ping its deter
mining path

into the va
cant realm

of those un
exposed water

ing-depths.

A real dove

sleekly self–

embracing
the coo-coo

ing of its
usual peace

ful call
tree-topped

to an invis
ibly unanswer

ing-futuring
realm.

A self-import

looking little

girl high-stepp
ed the gravell

ed stones of
her rearrang

ing thought-
climbs.

"Keeping up with

the times" left

him windless
ly inert until

he started tell
ing the time

s on his own
timeless

ly wind-invok
ing.

Minnowing

instant mo

ments where
they weren't

time-creat
ing fictive

ly sound
less.

A few ran

dom petals

fallen from a
flowering

bush somehow
creating a

sense of sad
ness as the

premature
death of a

child in the
midst of

summer's en
compassing

greenness.

A cat

perched a

top a sense
of avidly

waiting for
the appear

ance of its
unseen cause.

As a remind

er of Brahms'

Horn Trio
The refresh

ing call of
this early

morning breeze
to the lake'

s restless
ly uneasy in

creasing
ly response.

Aesop

fabled me

into a cat
and mouse

hide-out
world as a

Jew in dire
need of not-

being-found
out.

Sour grapes *(Aesop)*

They'll al

ways remain
(not only for

the clever ex
cuses of the

fox-in-us)
a higher be

yond-the-
reach of our

self-seeking
for more.

The lion' *(Aesop)*

s the stronger –

I'll take it
all-for-me

and leave the
others hungry

at the beggar'
s door reminds

us (so pain
fully now) of

those modern-
day lions

not yet caged-
into where

they so just
ly belong.

A spider

so microscop

ically small
that I couldn'

t quite imagine his
catching any

thing that
could hold in

an imaginary
net.

The whiten

ing steamer

adrifting
our far-out

thought
s waved-in

solitary re
sponse.

A little

girl with a

big-round
ball as if

holding the
whole of a

world in her
coloring

hands.

Late summer'

s shadows

diffusely
deepening

as sleep slow
ly merging

into those
untouch

able realm
s of night.

Those dis

tant mount
ains bared–

down from cen
turies of im

movably watch
ing as if

they themsel
ves had be

come the final
cause of a

lasting judg
ment.

Are these

down-wind

ing stair
s through

my scarce
ly percept

ible thought
s muted to

their fad
ing cloth-

touched e
choings.

That half-

faced morn

ing moon
skied into

a timeless
depth of blue

just hanging
there an ap

parition
of night'

s scarcely
perceptive

dreams.

It seems

as if the

winds have a
wakened these

morning-scent
ed flower

s to their
true-sense

of perpet
ual color

s.

Shutter

s down enclos

ing that scarce
ly-used-house

in the depth
of its own

evil-shadow
ings.

A bird

less leaf

less tree
awared of its

nakedly told
death–imagin

ings.

Those prehis

toric stones

sourcing
the shores of

this still–
contemplat

ing lake with
the deaf–numb

ness of an
cient–baring

times.

The heaven'

s light–toned–

blue as mild
as these soft

summer wind
s as if the

world here had
become trans

parently real
ized.

Wind-swept

phrasing

those sudden
ly–becoming

clouds hori
zoned beyond

whatever ill
uminating

light–curr
ents.

Even when

the night

had reached
its darkest

enclosure
s These white

gulls secret
ly passing

through Wingèd
to their

(as yet) in
decipher

able cause.

Different

he was from

the others al
ways remote

ly seated to
a big book

that seemed
to be turn

ing the hand-
touched page

s of his in
dwelling

life.

Kayak

ing repeat

ed even-sid
ed stroke

s as if keep
ing himself

balanced
to the wave'

s constant
ly rhythm

ic accord
s.

Out-of-

bounds un

touchably
remote those

high-borne
reeds nest

ing with the
scarcely

audible
cries of

baby bird
s not yet

rhymed to
the wave's

rhythmic
calling

s.

For Rosemarie

even the name

you so child
ly rejected

speaking only
of your myster

iously call
ing smile

that enveloped
me in the

comforting
ease of noth

ing more or
less than

only-now.

A tiny lizard

stone-cooled

hushed past
not a whisper

ing's worth.

Her off-

step walk

neither curr
ently moved

nor self–en
ticing but

with a char
acterist

ic almost
stuttering

moment of
self-aimed

sufficien
cy.

A parade

of swans

orderly
claiming

while
stream–lin

ed to its
mother

ly white
ness.

Under

ground root

s but no
tree in

sight as if
time had been

broken-off
here leading

to the no
where of soli

tary remain
s.

A poem

speaks for

itself
s the mea

sure of its
own meaning

s.

These contin

uous calling

of waves
and those in

nocent pleasu
re boats

self-decept
ively surfac

ing a lake
depthed in

to the realm
s of its un

told withhold
ing darkness

es.

Prettily

descriptive

lyrics are
like women

dressed in
light spring–

timed phras
es.

Transformings

The town

(in itself
but modest

ly attired)
now transform

ed into cele
brating row

s of fest
ive coloring

s.

Self-portrait

He turned

out wrong
not charted

as a boat
for tradit

ional route
s but as an

offside
player run

ning still
his own map

ed-out dis
tances.

Seeing

If we could

only see the
inside thought

s guarded
from view ra

ther than
those dress

ed appearan
ces routine

ly on dis
play.

He dream

ed a cool–

frighten
ing feeling

down below
the wood–plan

ked floor a
giant snake

sliding
through

its unseen
skin awaken

ing–untold
distanc

es.

In haste

Always in

haste he run
ning about so

much that e
ven his stead

ily persist
ent shadow

s had trouble
in catching–

up–on–him.

Tommy

grew in

to himself
as a cocoon

that couldn'
t be let

out from the
work that de

termined
his daily

person.

A white gull

high above

the reach of
thought-trans

forming these
early morning

winds into
their light–

soundless ap
pearance

s.

Morning

moon fading

from its
through-ap

pearing dark
nesses.

Denying age

He couldn'

t deny age
always list

ening harder
for voice–

securing
tight to

the stepped-
railings

Pained at
the sudden

pull of his
back But he

could write
against it

voicing prim
ed-for light.

Classical

landscape

The trees
trimmed to

a precision
ed cause

The grass
es freed

from their
wild-growth

Even the
weeds flower

ing in decept
ive appearan

ces as if man
could tame

his uproot
ing self-deny

ing instinct
s.

If I could

only be that
kind of duck

probing the
water's deep

without los
ing balance

from these
time-shift

ing waves.

A dead fish

floating

on the wa
ter's edge

its light-
streaking

now-dulled-
muted-dead

to the speed
of its

awakening
glance.

The theme

s may repeat

but their mean
ings continu

ally change
If they didn'

t time would
n't be turn

ing its kalaido
scopic view

or perhaps
I would just

be sitting
here as a log

too heavily
watering

down.

These early-

morning–riser
s watching

the sound of
the waves com

ing in as
phases of

their life
repeating

in restless
review of

the more-be
coming

s.

Spring Song' (Mendelssohn)

s slightly
sugar-coated

whimsical
feeling

s as prett
ily attired

young ladies
in the fin

eries of
their dress

ed-up trans
parent appear

ances.

Lizard

lithely

clinging
to the little

ness of its
sound-sens

ings.

A heat

so dense

that it dren
ched his

dreams in
to an image

less void.

The time

didn't stop

at its u
sual place

he slept
past it in

to those
timeless

ly vacant
shores of en

veloping
night.

For Rosemarie *(Stephen Foster)*

"Beautiful

dreamer" Rose
marie at 73

star-light
ing my mid–

night gazing
the full-

length of
her impercept

ible dream–ac
cords.

He's at the

camera now
She with the

kayak capsiz
ing her al

ways promin
ently photo

genic smile.

Down-days

One of those

down–days
in the shore

less silence
s of the seas

Hades with
out the oars

man yet time
fully prepar

ed.

Sick-days

It was only

on those sick-
days that he

rediscover
ed the length

and width of
his roomed–

in–thought
s The walls

those silent
barriers to

his not–gett
ing–out–from.

Voice-reminding

You can't

change the
tones of the

church–bell's
repeating

those same
declaring

sounds de
cades of end

lessly voice–
reminding.

Aesop'

s milk-maid

head-heavy
with dream

s dripping
down to their

floor-levell
ed waste.

Aesop'

s Land and City Mouse

Even for a
mouse in that

classical
land of cul

ture tast
ing the sim

ple ways of
outdoor freed

om's better-
off than the

refined joy
s of danger

ous city-
life.

16th century

Avila's

secret Walls
of a silence

strangely re
mote enclos

ing two Jewish
saints and

Victoria'
s music as

eternal as
man's long

ing for pur
ities of

sound.

The pier

reaching

its end at
the open–

sea lay be
yond untouch

ed by man'
s need to si

lence those
restless

waves press
ing so deep

ly within.

Baal

persisted

to taunt
man's un

touched de
sires and

the golden
calf shining

through Man
hattan's

statued–
liberty

(yet still)
those 10 comm

andments
stone-forgott

en remembr
ances.

Ghettoed

They may have

been ghettoed
dirtied liv

ing-the-fear
of worse to

come But still
they remained

self-sustain
ing a faith

candled in a
remote yet cen

turied light.

Still wave

s as if these

fears of time
s-to-come

could be so
easily wash

ed away unre
membered.

Writing a

gainst the

times classi
cally invoking

an aesthetic
of restrain

ed purity in
these eclectic

ally decadent
Mahlerian

times.

When does the

intrinsical

ly self-sus
taining evil

of an artist
indelibly

blemish his
work Wagner'

s the case
the answer'

s yours.

Middle-

aged decent

ly clothed
a compan

ionship that
seemed long–

harbored
for constant

and continu
al small-time

pleasure
s.

Bulldog'

s tensely–

leashed to
the rock-moun

ing over the
water's out

spreading in
herently self–

defiant cause.

The castle

at Sirmione

classical
ly bred equal

ly stoned
to its self–

enclosing
past.

The cliff

s of Sirmione's

ruins of those
down-spaced

times as shore–
lined guard

ians of those
still invisi

bly danger
s from with

in.

Early Schubert

quartet's

youthful
voice sound

ing above its
becoming

only-his.

Plumes

The fruit'
s ripening

almost to
the feel of

its tasting
fullness

Coloring
deeply into

autumn's har
vesting plea

sures.

Irene

that hurri

cane as if
aimed right–

up the Eastern
Seaboard clean

sing not only
those abandon

ed streets
of their one–

time tower
ing "imper

ial" claim
s.

Sleep wander

er through

those time
less realms

of moon's
dense-phan

toming
s.

Flower

s holding
fast to what

these fin
gers told of

their first–
coloring im

pulses.

Puzzled

If words

don't quite
fit their pre–

accustomed
place the puz

zle's never
inbecoming

complete.

Cool lake-

stream's

stirred sur
facing the

summer's
last reflect

ively timed–ap
pearance

s.

Radiatings

The heavy

splash of a
fully-sized

fish's un
seen colors

radiating
through the

expanding
waves of its

outreaching
source.

For Alena *(age 10)*

She couldn'

t imagine a
picture with

out being per
soned however

the landscape
kept telling

her the touch
ed contour

s of its
time-evok

ing self.

The Schubert

(even those

early quar
tets) modu

lating as
softly as the

touch of mall
eable clay–

forming
s.

Must we

learn through

others to
find those

only-intonat
ions of our

own self-voi
cings.

Classical *(in defense of Haydn)*

only when

the less be
comes more

of each tone
still waken

ing-alive.

The flow of

these poetic

lines weaving
into the in

tricacie
s of pre-de

signed
thought-

waves.

The Wind

s sourced

in their
self-resolv

ing inquiet
udes.

They

weren't fly

ing too high
to know who

they were
(mostly Jews)

We thought
of them as

our special
friends until

25 years later
when we knew

what they knew
They could

have bombed
them with

costly ammuni
tion? War–time

needs come
first? (they

were only Jew
s anyway).

And now we'

    ll be left a

    lone again
    (excuses

    come later)
    Falsing the

    facts of '48
    Our special friend

    s and only a
    God watching

    (as they
    mean) from

    perhaps too–
    far–above?

Going deaf

    a world cut–

    off silent
    ly abandon

    ed only those
    speechless

    walls listen
    ing back as

    hard as they
    only could.

Afrodite-Vittoria Brescia *(3ʳᵈ C. BC)*

Those space

less eyes in
folding hair

contemplat
ing a beauty

beyond man'
s smoothly–

felt word
less aware

nesses.

A single

small sun
flower imi

tating the
lessening

effort of
warmth sum

mer ly ease.

55 years later

she would
have sent him

away to a no–
returning

to taunt her
patient

less unease
How far that

would have
been 55 years

later from a
poetic vis

ion lost in
fathomless

self–fear
s.

A little

person of
common truth

s She alway
s remained

close to what
she saw (e

ven the pin
s and needle

s) But not the
distance

s of what be
came so vast

ly beyond her
breadth-of–

view.

He alway

s knew more

what he didn'
t want to be

lieve as if
playing the

unbeliev
ing fool of

life-enchant
ing self-de

ception
s.

For my Mother

If love is
the Christ-re

deeming truth
and humor's

that pungent
every-day

means of her
becoming

that more of
even in

our love-marr
iage of 50

years.

These shift

ing cloud-ton

alities evas
ively mirror

ing a world
set loose

from its own
securing-

hold.

Günter Grass

hiding in

the secur
ing comfort

from his own
N. S. past

while moral
izing away

those other
s who could

n't anymore.

"The conscien

ce of a nation'

s" only that
unveiling

voice gnaw
ing at the

very-depth
of one's own

hide-out
guilt.

For Rosemarie

Love was

never earn
ed though al

ways given
secretly

pearl-enclos
ed in the

depth of our
own pentrat

ing oyster
ed self.

St. Paul and

Luther focus

ing square
ly the where

of where
there's a

nowhere
s out from

those dark
ly encompass

ing self-sha
dowings.

An off-

flowered

secluded
place where

weeds pos
ing innocent

ly imitat
ing an o

ther's
source-from-

being.

These un

   even wind

   s flourish
   ing that

   little boy'
   s kite in

   to the color
   ings of his

   dreamed-imag
   ination

   s.

The sales

   man's voice

   so softly
   self-effac

   ing that I
   feared his

   eyes would
   melt if

   seen too-
   closely

   through.

Cultured

land order

ed and refin
ed the grass

es cut down
to their ex

pressive
scent the

trees just–
rightly plac

ed defining
each other’

s realm for
growth Only

man seems un
able to order

himself to
a perpetual

blossoming
fruitful

ness.

Tiny bird

tree-topped

to a slender
ing touch

ed–moment
arily air

ed-for-view.

2nd *Commandment* (Moses)

If
so many of

the great
artists pain

ted the theme
s colors and

distance
s of their

realizing faith
Why do art

historian
s mostly

paint a pic
ture of them

in the image
of their own

agnostic
denial.

Strauss-Kahn

He may have

suddenly ap
peared as na

ked as when
The Lord had

first clothed
him Jumped out

on her as a
tiger hungry

for the flesh
of his own

self–devour
ing instinct

s.

The scent

of September'

s distant
potato fire'

s stone de
ciphering

yet vague
ly remote.

Biltmore Hotel (1942)

the only time

my sister
felt our fa

ther's so
deeply hurt

Crying over
the massacre

of Jews but
also the rich

American one
s who weren'

t prepared to
help – accessor

ies to those
crimes their

lost identity
money-minded

ness the meas
ure of all

their paper
ing achieve

ments.

Street

light's glass–

imagining
the depth of

those untouch
ed darken

ing silenc
es.

Edith Stein

Did she die

by becoming
a Catholic

martyrer
or because of

her Jewish
blood that flow

ed as Christ'
s into an i

dentity of
always-their

s.

A tree on

a branch–

leafed to
the touch of

wind–invoking
remembran

ces Now stump
ed to its

earth–near out–
rooted ex

posures.

Joseph

Roth's pur

ity of sound–
phrasing

his careful
ly classi

cal intent
against

the overflow
of wine in

habiting
his mid–night

word–swells.

"Aryan"

book-burning
s – Can

one burn the
printed word

out-of the
mind of their

ash–blood
resolving i

dentitie
s.

I believe

in the wholly

Christian
church rather

than a narrow-
streamed credo

emancipat
ing from their

root's deep
er-earthed.

The cemetery

seemed more

like an assem
bly of still-

aging stone'
s time–gather

ings.

Isaiah 53

Were the

Jew's guilt –
sacrifi

ced for us –
all Or was

it the real
izing truth

of their un
known Christ-

calling
s.

Poetry books by David Jaffin

1. **Conformed to Stone,** Abelard-Schuman, New York 1968, London 1970.

2. **Emptied Spaces,** with an illustration by Jacques Lipschitz, Abelard-Schuman, London 1972.

3. **In the Glass of Winter,** Abelard-Schuman, London 1975, with an illustration by Mordechai Ardon.

4. **As One,** The Elizabeth Press, New Rochelle, N. Y. 1975.

5. **The Half of a Circle,** The Elizabeth Press, New Rochelle, N. Y. 1977.

6. **Space of,** The Elizabeth Press, New Rochelle, N. Y. 1978.

7. **Preceptions,** The Elizabeth Press, New Rochelle, N. Y. 1979.

8. **For the Finger's Want of Sound,** Shearsman Plymouth, England 1982.

9. **The Density for Color,** Shearsman Plymouth, England 1982.

10. **Selected Poems** with an illustration by Mordechai Ardon, English/Hebrew, Massada Publishers, Givatyim, Israel 1982.

11. **The Telling of Time,** Shearsman, Kentisbeare, England 2000 and Johannis, Lahr, Germany.

12. **That Sense for Meaning,** Shearsman, Kentisbeare, England 2001 and Johannis, Lahr, Germany.

13. **Into the timeless Deep,** Shearsman, Kentisbeare, England 2003 and Johannis, Lahr, Germany.

14. **A Birth in Seeing,** Shearsman, Exeter, England 2003 and Johannis, Lahr, Germany.

15. **Through Lost Silences,** Shearsman, Exeter, England 2003 and Johannis, Lahr, Germany.

16. **A voiced Awakening,** Shearsman, Exter, England 2004 and Johannis, Lahr, Germany.

17. **These Time-Shifting Thoughts**, Shearsman, Exeter, England 2005 and Johannis, Lahr, Germany.

18. **Intimacies of Sound,** Shearsman, Exeter, England 2005 and Johannis, Lahr, Germany.

19. **Dream Flow** with an illustration by Charles Seliger, Shearsman, Exeter, England 2006 and Johannis, Lahr, Germany.

20. **Sunstreams** with an illustration by Charles Seliger, Shearsman, Exeter, England 2007 and Johannis, Lahr, Germany.

21. **Thought Colors,** with an illustration by Charles Seliger, Shearsman, Exeter, England 2008 and Johannis, Lahr, Germany.

22. **Eye-Sensing,** Ahadada, Tokyo, Japan and Toronto, Canada 2008.

23. **Wind-phrasings,** with an illustration by Charles Seliger, Shearsman, Exeter, England 2009 and Johannis, Lahr, Germany.

24. **Time shadows,** with an illustration by Charles Seliger, Shearsman, Exeter, England 2009 and Johannis, Lahr, Germany.

25. **A World mapped-out,** with an illustration by Charles Seliger, Shearman, Exeter, England 2010.

26. **Light Paths,** with an illustration by Charles Seliger, Shearsman, Exeter, England 2011.

27. **Always Now,** with an illustration by Charles Seliger, Shearsman, Bristol, England 2011 and Edition Wortschatz, Schwarzenfeld, Germany.

Book on David Jaffin's poetry: Warren Fulton, **Poemed on a beach,** Ahadada, Tokyo, Japan and Toronto, Canada 2010.